The
Athletic
Horse

The Athletic Horse

Building on strengths, overcoming weaknesses

Horst Becker

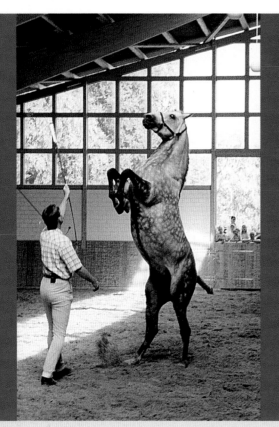

'Focusing my horse's
concentration on me...
Channelling his courage, power
and elegance...
Harnessing his temperament,
but not stifling it...
Shaping the horse, without misshaping him
Become one with my horse...–
All this is what dressage means to me'

Horst Becker

Copyright © 2007 by Cadmos Verlag GmbH, Schwarzenbek, Germany
Copyright of this edition © 2010 by Cadmos Books, Great Britain
Design and setting: Ravenstein + Partner, Verden.
Cover and content photos: Christiane Slawik
Drawings: Julia Denmann, Maria Mähler
Editor: Anneke Bosse
Translation: Claire Williams
Printed by: Westermann Druck, Zwickau
All rights reserved.

Printed in Germany

ISBN 978-3-86127-976-1

Contents

Contents

Thoughts on this book

Dear readers,

The reason for me writing this book is primarily because the problems identified during a horse's training are either not properly recognised, or are wrongly interpreted. The question 'Why' is rarely even posed. Why does a horse refuse to do a certain exercise? Why does he avoid another? Or why won't he take up a steady contact? This book should help to answer some of these questions, and to find easier ways to solve these problems in order to overcome some of the basic weaknesses found in many horses.

Many riders try to solve these problems by using brute strength. This method can only lead to a dead end. Or, to quote Egon von Neindorff: 'Where ability ends, force begins.'

The following points mirror my basic belief that for long-term success, a horse must be trained in such a way that is fair to the horse. The contents of these paragraphs have become my guiding principles when training both horses and riders, and in my view are an important basis for anyone who would like to work with horses and has an appreciation, understanding and respect for their well-being.

• Horses are not pieces of sports equipment. They are creatures with a soul, with feelings, and above all else, with a memory. They never forget what they have learnt, but they also remember when force has been used in a particular lesson – which may cause them to panic when they are even faintly reminded of it.

• Horses do not stand in their stables or out in the field for twenty-three hours a day, thinking about ways they can irritate their rider when they turn up to ride them. Horses that are more outwardly focused – such as those that shy frequently or that won't concentrate on their work – are often not happy in themselves. It would be like you going to the gym with a bad back or having to look after a horde of screaming children when you have a migraine.

• Horses tend to suffer silently for a long time before it even occurs to the rider that something might be wrong. Often, a rider gets a feeling that something isn't quite right – but the instructor doesn't take it seriously and instead says 'ride him more forwards, he's just being lazy and you need

to be more assertive!' Of course you don't want to be taken advantage of, but you owe it to your horse, as a living being, to ask yourself whether you or he is the source of the problem. I have been riding since I was eleven years old and have been training horses and riders for 15 years, and have rarely met a horse that didn't want to, but many who couldn't.

• Once you are on the right track in your training, you can feel and see this in the horse's enjoyment and satisfaction, and in the harmonious way he moves. Horses are herd animals, and for them we are their herd leader. A horse will always try to integrate himself into the herd wherever possible.

• Horses are performance athletes – runners, dancers and high jumpers. They have strengths and weaknesses that a rider has to work with.

• Schooling a horse consists primarily of gaining his trust, building up reliable lines of communication and above all, preparing him physically so that he is able to carry a person on his back and to fulfil all of the demands made of him.

I have saved both yourself and myself by not repeating things in this book that other excellent horsemen and women have already written about numerous times before. This book is the result of eight years of analysis, experimentation and further analysis – as well as innumerable drafts.

I have often asked myself whether my thoughts are even worth putting down on paper. In this context I would like to thank all those who have supported me in doing it 'my way': Fredy Knie Sr. and Prof. Kurt Albrecht, both of whom are sadly no longer alive – I would so much have liked to have presented both of them with a copy of this book. They gave me the necessary tools to understand classical dressage properly, and were always my inspiration. They often supported me with help and advice to keep me from straying from the path of classical dressage, but also encouraged me to be open and look at things from a different angle. I have often viewed these two people as the 'Last of the Mohicans' – as they firmly believed in 'their classical dressage' but were never stuffy or stubborn, instead being open to new methods that could help both horse and rider. On the other hand, they always responded with categorical dismissal when anything was based on force, outbursts of temper or egotism.

I would also like to thank Detlef Rittman: he was the first person who was able to answer my questions on biomechanics linked with riding and allowed me, so to speak, to look at his cards. In doing so he helped a simple rider and instructor like me to understand this connection and put it into practice.

I would also like to, and indeed must, thank my pupils who have helped to show me over the past years, through theirs and their horses' own efforts, what the right way has been. And also for being honest with me about their successes and failures with respect to my instruction, as only then can a trainer find out what is the right way for the individual horse and rider.

These days the Scales of Training (as laid out by the German Equestrian Federation) are always used as a guideline for the rider when schooling his horse. But these Scales describe only what you can see and perhaps feel, and not what you need to do or how you need to do it. For me the

physical and mental state of the horse is important in training the horse as an athlete – in other words strength, balance, rhythm, suppleness, obedience to the aids, complete calm and self-confidence. It is these things that need to be worked on together so that you can achieve rhythm, suppleness, relaxedness and impulsion.

I hope that this book gives you new ideas for your work with your horse and gives you some enthusiasm for trying some new approaches well as old and classical methods. Out of respect for our horses and out of thanks for the many incredibly enjoyable hours spent in the saddle, we should never stop learning or trying to improve our understanding.

Horst Becker, March 2007

Considering horse **biomechanics** with regard to training

Once a human athlete's talent has been discovered, it is carefully and strategically developed. The four-legged athlete, on the other hand, is often more experimentally trained. This method is not only less effective, but can also at times have negative consequences, from the horse becoming supposedly and inexplicably uncooperative, through to showing early signs of wear and tear, and even becoming totally unrideable.

Balanced movement is a motivation in itself.

The first steps

The search for harmony in movement – this perfect union of horse and rider – is in physical terms impossible, and yet in certain respects horse and rider can melt into one if the horse is able to move in a balanced and contained manner.

Fredy Knie always used to say when teaching that the horse needed to go 'on the bit and into the leg'. It is precisely the phrase 'into the leg' that bes describes the above goal of harmony between horse and rider. Once a horse has loosened and relaxed his body completely, it will appear to the rider that his legs and seat sink into the horse, and merge together to become as one.

One of the most important basic prerequisites for this is finding the correct tempo – most riders usually ride at too fast a pace. Only when the horse can propel himself from back to front, i.e. push through from his quarters with this impulsion going through his entire body, can a horse be truly balanced from within. This requires the rider to have a relaxed knee so that the horse's shoulder isn't blocked, and a seat that is balanced slightly forwards. The so-called deep seat and the tendency to want to concertina the horse underneath the rider can throttle, in the true sense of the word, a horse's motivation to want to move and be in balance with his rider.

There are two sensible ways to start schooling a horse:

1. When the horse has a steady consistent movement, the quality of the contact is of secondary importance – in time this will usually improve by itself. If you decide you need to work on this, because often in competition the horse's outline is scored more highly than a horse that is moving willingly forwards in balance, then take great care that this natural freedom of movement is not interfered with.

2. When a horse has not got such a naturally free movement it is important that he becomes noticeably and visibly rounder and more contained in his carriage and outline. When I speak of carriage and outline, then I don't just mean the horse's head and neck, but his entire body. At the same time, the 'how' and 'when' of any adjustments is of great significance for the success or otherwise of the training. To better understand how the horse works it is important that you learn how his musculoskeletal system functions.

A perfect demonstration of balance in movement.

The principles
of biomechanics

One of the most important principles of classical dressage is that 'the rider must always ensure that his horse never falls onto the forehand.'

If we look at a horse's skeleton then we can see that the bone structure of the forehand is clearly stronger, and therefore heavier, than that of the hindquarters and that the centre of gravity of the entire skeleton will therefore clearly lie closer to the forehand. This places the statement demanding that a horse should 'never' be allowed to go on his forehand in a questionable light. The same conclusion is reached when you consider the horse's entire musculature: the forehand – including his head and neck – is more strongly muscled and therefore heavier then the hindquarters.

You therefore have to ask yourself how this requirement that the horse should carry his weight through his quarters has come into being.

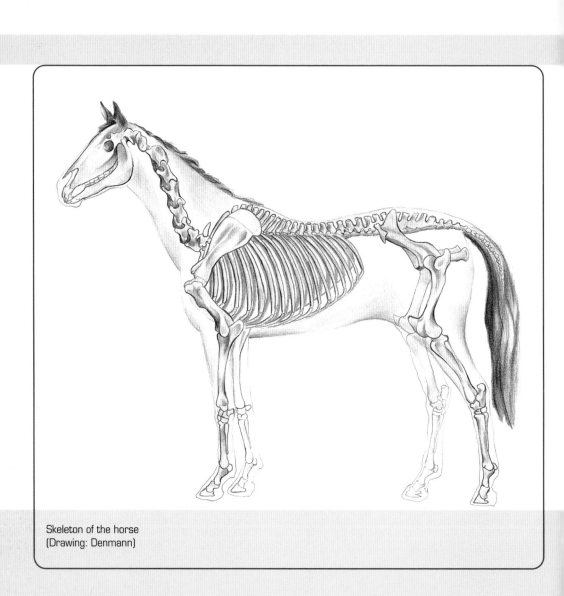

Skeleton of the horse
(Drawing: Denmann)

Of course, by this we do not mean that, for example, the horse should carry 400 kg through his hindquarters and 200 kg on his forehand, but rather that whichever hindleg is moving forwards will be moving through and under him as far forwards as possible, underneath his centre of gravity. In doing so, the hindlegs will be carrying the entire weight of the horse's body in this forwards movement for a longer period of time. The prerequisite for this is that the muscles of the back and quarters are both relaxed and have the ability to stretch so that the hindleg can step through and reach far forwards. In addition, the muscles in the legs, stomach and back must be developed enough to be able to carry weight for a decent period of time.

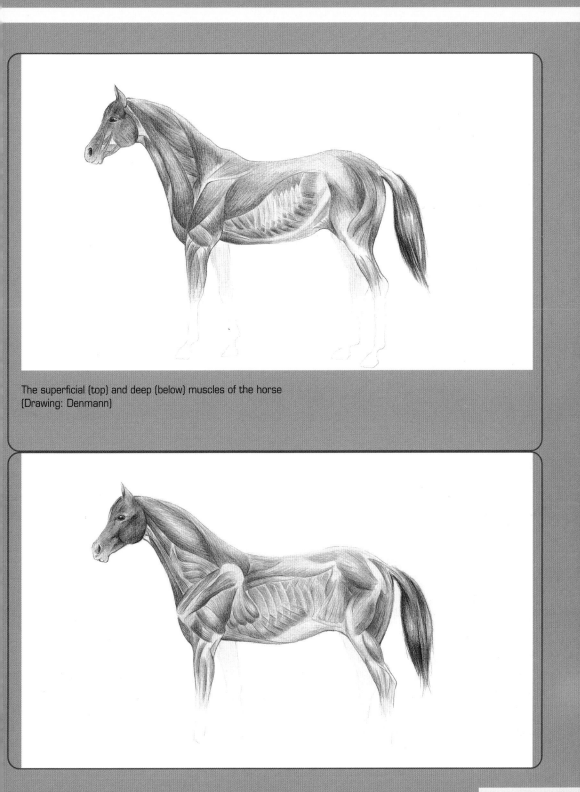

The superficial (top) and deep (below) muscles of the horse
(Drawing: Denmann)

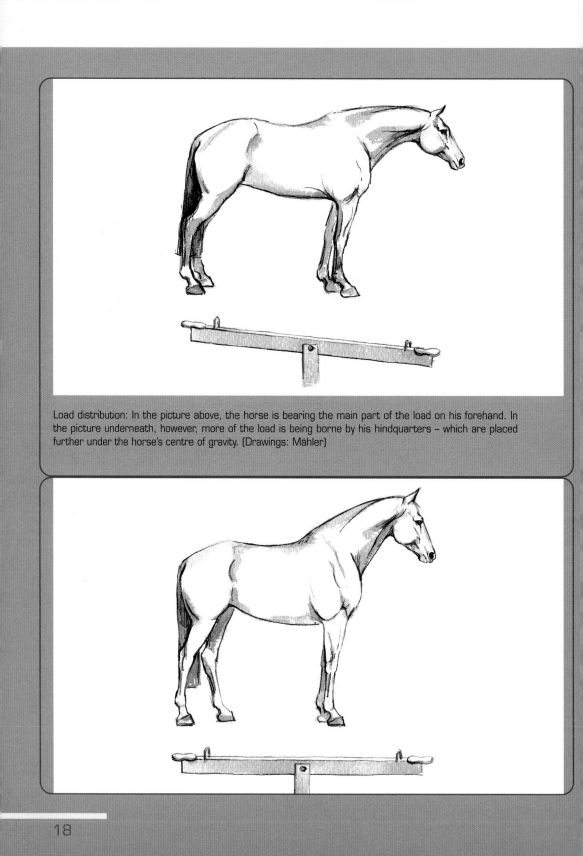

Load distribution: In the picture above, the horse is bearing the main part of the load on his forehand. In the picture underneath, however, more of the load is being borne by his hindquarters – which are placed further under the horse's centre of gravity. (Drawings: Mähler)

The horse's ability to bend

When I ask a rider on which rein her horse is easier to work, she will usually answer, for example, that at walk and trot he is better on the left rein, but in canter he is better on the right. When the horse is ridden in walk and trot on the right rein, he will have problems with the lateral bend and in staying on a contact. On the left rein in canter, the horse is likely to take smaller strides and will tend to fall out through his shoulder to the right and may be disunited when striking off.

Previously I would have said that the horse described above should be worked more on the right rein so that he learns to bend more to the right. In terms of training his muscles though, this would have catastrophic results, because the rider's supposed own feeling being deceived: the left rein is not the horse's better side. It is more an issue that muscles on the left side are shorter so the horse will go slightly hollow to the left, looks for the contact on the left rein and will therefore feel comfortable in walk and trot. On the right rein, due to the shorter muscles, he will still be hollow to the left despite being flexed to the right by his rider. He is therefore put out of balance, and will fight against the contact and – since he needs to use his head to balance himself and can't stretch as well to the right – will instead try to flex to the left.

At a canter it is a different matter. If running is to the trot stride what jumping is for the canter stride, here he will be jumping through and around the circle. In this case, bending through the ribs is not as important for the quality of the canter as is the length and quality of each individual stride. Since, for the horse in our example, the left hand musculature in his quarters is shortened, then the canter strides on the left rein will be shorter and stiffer. As a result, the rider will have the feeling that the bad side – here the left in walk and trot – is good, although in canter it will be clear that the rider's feeling isn't reflecting reality, since here the right rein will be better.

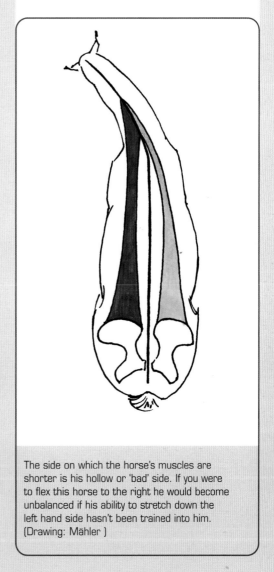

The side on which the horse's muscles are shorter is his hollow or 'bad' side. If you were to flex this horse to the right he would become unbalanced if his ability to stretch down the left hand side hasn't been trained into him. (Drawing: Mähler)

When warming up a horse like this, you would ride on the left rein in walk and trot first of all, but on the right rein you should first of all start off in canter in order to work his strengths and weaknesses in the best way possible. In the case of some of my horses, I would warm them up and work them for up to 90 per cent of the training session on his hollow side without changing the rein. The easier a horse is to warm up and get supple then the earlier I am likely to change the rein.

Shortened muscles can't be lengthened just by stretching them directly. Instead they have to be warmed up and made more supple by using them – in other words, by contracting and relaxing them.

The three muscle chains

• The withers and back: centre of movement
The withers are the key to movement. Only when the withers are open, like a Spanish senorita's fan, can a horse really move fluidly. A horse can only

In canter it is the length of the individual stride and the way it is carried out more than his ability to bend through his ribs that are the decisive factors for the quality of the canter.

Ligaments connect the poll with the withers. If a horse drops his head and neck down, then the ligaments pull the withers forwards and open. (Drawing: Mähler)

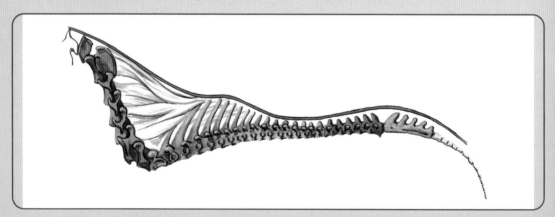

move rhythmically and with cadence when his back swings, just as the forehand can really only be raised and become lighter once the withers are opened.

There are two ways in which a horse might open his withers: one is by using his muscles, of which more later, and one that is more mechanical, involving ligaments.

I can best describe this by giving you an example. A rider works his horse at walk and trot for 30 – 45 minutes. The horse becomes more relaxed, dropping his head and neck down and into a contact. The rider now thinks that his horse is warmed up and can really start to work him. In reality, though, the horse has dropped his head and neck because he is tired and the power in his quarters is now not sufficient to keep his back rounded and his withers open.

• The hindquarters: the power house

Once the withers are opened it is easier for the hindquarters to step underneath, since when the hindleg reaches forwards, the resistance from the back and withers lessens and allows the abdominal muscles to work more effectively. Compared to the back muscles, the abdominal muscles are much too weak to cause a horse to overtrack properly if the back muscles are stiff and the withers are closed.

The hindquarters of the horse can be likened to the motor of car, and provide the power and the control. The muscles of the hindquarters, back and stomach – when combined – contribute towards the creation of movement. When taken individually they work like this: the contraction of the abdominal muscles causes the back to round, allowing the hindleg that is taking a step forwards to be placed well underneath the horse into his centre of gravity, providing that at the moment when the leg is

Perfect cadence in motion can only occur when the withers are opened.

swinging forwards the muscles of the back and hindquarters are loose. If the hindleg has been put down onto the ground, taking up the horse's weight, again the muscles in the back and quarters will contract, creating the forwards motion of the horse's body providing there is sufficient bend through the haunches.

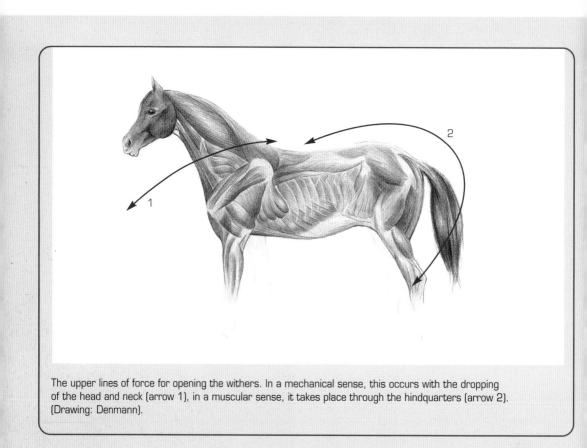

The upper lines of force for opening the withers. In a mechanical sense, this occurs with the dropping of the head and neck (arrow 1), in a muscular sense, it takes place through the hindquarters (arrow 2). (Drawing: Denmann).

If the tempo set by the rider is too fast, then the hindleg stays in action too long and will be left behind. Because of this, the back will be arched downwards through the loins. As a result, his stomach muscles won't be as quick to round the back to allow for his other hindleg to move through, thus the horse's movement will start to deteriorate.

To an inexperienced eye, a horse's forehand may look more spectacular at a greater 'speed', which explains why so many horses are ridden too fast. There is a big difference between a horse that will just go faster and one that can truly come through from behind when asked for

more extension. From the point of view of biomechanics, the two are totally different things.

If the correct tempo and rhythm is adhered to, then the initial hindleg will not stay so long in the phase when it pushes off from the ground, the loins won't sink down so extremely and the abdominal muscles are able to round up the back again to initiate the action of the second hindleg. The result is that the horse stays compact, doesn't become strung out and steps through cleanly from behind.

If a horse's back isn't loose – because of tension caused by either over-exertion or a poorly-fitting saddle – then the abdominal muscles cannot work effectively. If the saddle is too long or placed too

When the pace is too fast, the leg that is pushing off stays on the ground too long and causes the back to arch down.

If the back is rounded then the abdominal muscles can work without interference and the hindleg can step through well underneath the horse.

far back then it will rest on the start of the muscles in the hindquarters. This will result in tension in these muscles too, and the hindleg will not be able to step through far enough because it will be held back by the gluteal muscles in the hindquarters. Simply put, it means that the quarters are tensed at the wrong time. This is found often with Icelandic ponies and sometimes with horses being ridden in a Western saddle.

If the withers aren't open because the horse's head is held too high or the saddle is too narrow – and this is a frequent reason for a horse going above the bit – then there is too much resistance occurring when the hindleg swings forwards, meaning that it can't step through enough under the centre of gravity. If you work the horse deeper, asking him to drop his head, then the action of the head and neck will help to open the withers.

If you want to build up a muscle then you should work it repeatedly using only a small amount of weight for as long as possible but not far enough to overexert it. By overexerting it you would strain the muscle, which could lead to tearing it, potentially restricting and even stopping any sustained attempt to the process of developing the muscle. Or, to put it another way, if you go the gym, you do many repetitions of an exercise with a small weight, and not each exercise once with a heavy weight.

• **Head and neck: the horse's balancing pole**

The head and neck is the balancing pole as well as the mirror of your horse's physical fitness. You can see from his neck whether a horse is being properly ridden or whether he is being held together by gadgets such as side- or running- reins, as well as seeing what stage of his training he is at. It is only when a horse stands in his stable in a similar way to how he looks when being ridden – with a degree of containment and self-carriage – that his body is fit and able to take the demands of constant work.

All rider problems are reflected in the way the horse carries himself – directly, in the case of either the rough or unpredictable influence of the rider, or indirectly, when the horse loses his balance during an exercise, due to, for example, being ridden too quickly. A poorly-fitting saddle will also be revealed in a horse's neck – more about this later.

What happens within a horse when he mouths on the bit?

In equestrian circles, the action of a horse mouthing on the bit is a synonym for good training or well being, although it can be conjured up with tricks such as a piece of mane knotted into the bit or by using a bit flavoured with apple. None of these tricks help to advance a rider's ability however, but instead hide the real problem.

The poll is the key to opening the withers: if a horse goes along with his teeth clenched, then the poll will also be tense and the rider has little chance of getting the horse to listen to his finely tuned aids through the hand and rein. This is, however, the prerequisite for a refined method of training, and in the end for the horse giving trustingly to the rein and working into the hand.

This Friesian is moving with an open back and shoulder and is using his abdominal muscles.

Due to the tensed muscles underneath his neck the horse's back is being pressed down.

The raised inner hand directly effects the corner of the horse's mouth, not the tongue.

When the horse gives and drops his head, the hand is lowered.

Here is the sting in the tail: if a horse does not give to the rein then the rider can't form the horse's body into the shape required for the horse to then find the work easier and loosen up through his back. If his back is tense or stiff then so is his poll.

We have to break this vicious circle – our tool for this is in riding with a raised inside hand. By doing this the rider opens the way to a new level of sensitivity in his riding in terms of the influence they have on the horse. At the same time as being seen as good, it is also seen as dangerous and for this reason is much debated. On the one hand, the corner of the mouth is pulled up with the bit and the horse answers with a similar pressure downwards which at the beginning of his training is where we want his head to be.

On the other hand, the effect of taking the rein up takes the pressure off the horse's tongue. This causes the horse to release the lower neck muscles which prevents the horse's back rounding up correctly or opening his withers. It is the tongue however that is at the top end of a muscular chain reaction which ends at the sternum.

If the horse accepts the raised hand then he will open his mouth a little as long as the noseband isn't done up too tightly. If he starts to mouth on the bit and drop his head at this stage, then providing you are working at a tempo that is appropriate for the horse's stage of physical development, you should already start to see and feel improvements within the pace. The horse will appear more contained and be rounder in his movement, and the rider will feel as if he is being carried along more easily and have a better overall feeling. I will talk more about the use of this aid later. But a word of caution: you must not concentrate on the inside rein and forget about the outside rein, as this only reinforces the argument of those who criticise this method and makes correct riding impossible. Riding with both hands raised should be left to the experts as you have to counter the missing outside support with correct driving aids through the seat and leg; otherwise, you may have a well shaped neck but at the same time a hollow back and quarters that are dragging. The rider's balance can also be affected, in that he tips backwards and hangs onto the reins so that he can't relax either his stomach or back.

If you try to ride your horse into a lower outline by using draw-reins, then you are achieving exactly the opposite of what a raised inner hand does. The increased pressure on the horse's tongue causes the horse to look, at least in most cases, as if he is working through the poll. From a biomechanical point of view though, it is totally different: the pressure on the tongue causes the muscles on the underside of the neck to contract. Since this pressure works downwards and backwards the horse will exert a counter pressure forwards and upwards, which in turn increases the pressure on the horse's tongue.

Pressure on the tongue causes the horse to tense up his lower neck muscles and exert a counter pressure which causes him to hollow his back even more. Bottom: when a horse has a softer mouth and is working through from behind, then he will work with a relaxed and swinging back. (Drawings: Mähler)

If you look at the poll of this horse more carefully from the side, you will see how the parotid salivary gland is squashed up between his jaw bone and the tensed neck muscle, which can lead to a very painful infection. Or to understate the issue – the horse will look like he is thick through the throat which is in most cases ridiculous, as he wouldn't if he was ridden correctly.

Due to the muscles fighting against the pressure caused by the draw-reins, the horse's neck muscles will develop in the wrong way. (Drawings: Mähler)

But staying on the topic of draw-reins, how do you recognise if a horse has been ridden roughly with draw reins? Easily. If you are in the saddle looking at the line of the neck from the withers to the poll and the neck looks wider nearer the poll than at the shoulder, this is due to the poll continuously fighting against this pressure, and the withers never truly being opened. It would be correct if the neck came out of a wide shoulder and narrowed into the poll.

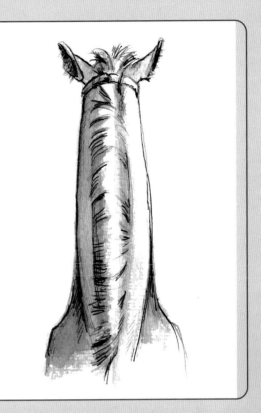

This is how the neck of a correctly trained horse should look from a rider's perspective and from the side. (Drawings: Mähler)

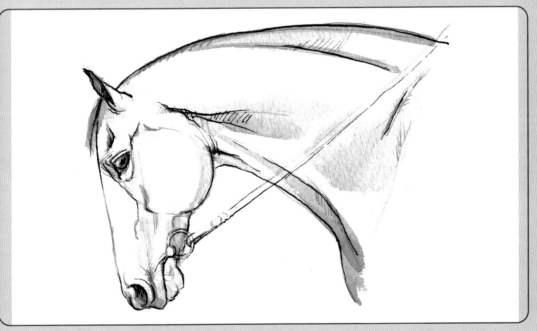

A well-fitting saddle

Eighty per cent of all problems experienced by riders are rooted in a poorly-fitted saddle. Often, the rider will have already taken action and called in an expert who will have supposedly adjusted the

This saddle is too narrow and, as a result, its lowest point is too far back.

Here the saddle is shown in the correct position.

saddle to fit, or has sold a new one that often doesn't fit either, or appears not to fit properly after a short while. This often happens because the saddle fitter doesn't know enough about riding and isn't aware of how much a horse can change shape during his training. Most saddlers or saddle fitters will do their best to fit a horse with a suitable saddle but they don't have the right picture in mind when choosing or fitting the saddle.

The most frequent case is that the saddle is too narrow in front. If the gullet plate at the front of the tree is too narrow then firstly the forehand, or rather the shoulder, will be pinched so that the withers can no longer open and will block any bend through the ribs because the outside shoulder muscle can't stretch. The result is that the horse can't bend. If the saddle is so narrow that it lies higher at the pommel than the cantle then this clearly has more dramatic consequences for horse and rider:

• The deepest part of the saddle, where the rider is supposed to sit, is no longer in the centre and is instead moved further back so that the rear part of the saddle is pressed into the horse's back. Since this part of the back is the part that moves the most, the cadence and quality of movement will be affected and become clearly restricted. Since the fan-like shoulder muscle is pinched, the horse may start to nod with his head.

• Due to the back half of the saddle having more weight in it, the front half will be lighter and may lift up off the shoulder. This may result in it slipping forwards onto the shoulder, meaning that the movement in the front legs comes from the legs only, and not through the shoulder. The pace will therefore lose expression and the quarters will drag. Often the horse will come right off the contact because his back muscles cannot relax. The result is a back that can't swing with the movement, and hindlegs that can't track up.

> A saddle that is too narrow will always slip forwards. If the saddle is too wide, then it will fall behind the shoulder and be pushed back by the bones in the shoulder. This often results in an apparently inexplicable lameness.

In the case of saddles used on breeds that tölt or pace, such as Icelandic ponies, then the problem is much worse since the saddles are not only too narrow in front but also placed too far back. The muscles in the group are always tensed and the horse will not step through under himself, because he can only do this when his muscles are relaxed. The picture that results of the horse's movement is one that makes the hindquarters look as if a part has broken down, and often horses are labelled as a-rhythmical or will be diagnosed with a lameness that can of course not successfully be treated, as the horse isn't actually lame. The owner then sets off on a long odyssey, because after a while this problem in his movement will persist even when the saddle is taken off. This is because the injury to the horse's bone and muscle structure will be so great that, without special treatment and training – which will include the work of a good physiotherapist – it may not be possible to fix.

In addition, there are further reasons for a saddle not fitting correctly:

• The gullet is too narrow: this doesn't occur as often now as it used to, because most saddle makers have changed the measurements they use in production. Should this be the case, then it becomes most obvious when riding small circles, when the horse has to bend. In a circle to the right, the right panel will be closer to the spine than the left and when there is not enough room between the two panels in tight turns or circles there will be pressure on the spine. Since this area is very sensitive to pressure, the horse will try to get his back away from this and will come off the contact. This will be easy to identify, because in larger circles the distance between the panels is sufficient and the horse will only come off the contact in very small circles.

• The saddle sits correctly and is also not too narrow, but despite this it keeps slipping forward onto the shoulder. Firstly, this may be due to the middle of the saddle being the only part making contact with the horse's back. When the horse lifts his back then he will lift the saddle over the shoulder so that it is sitting as if it were too narrow in front. The second possibility could be that the horse has a substantial grass belly (which, by the way, can only be the case for poorly-trained horses since then the abdominal muscles are too weak to keep the tummy trim) and the girth is slipping forwards behind the elbow. The saddle will then become loose and can't be kept in the right position. This can really only happen when the horse also has a very round shoulder. The solution here is to give the horse more exercise and put him on a diet. And finally, the saddle may also slip forwards when the horse is stiff through the back and/or bucks. This happens more in canter than in trot.

Besides this, the saddle has to fit the rider: not only does the seat have to be the right size, but

Two riders, one saddle? It just can't work when the difference in size is so large.

A small rider in a large saddle will feel like she is sitting on a Harley Davidson. Her legs will always slip forwards because the stirrup bars are too far away from the centre of the seat. This happens very frequently so it is often the case that when a rider's leg is too far forwards, it's not due to a lack of ability but rather down to the equipment. Just as with a horse, the rider's flexor and extensor muscles have to be in balance. If, as a rider, you have to constantly move your leg back, then the flexor muscles found in your leg and bottom are tensed and you don't have a chance of being balanced. This will have an effect on your seat, especially on how relaxed or loose it is, as well as your stamina. In this example your body is more likely to tip back and you will have problems staying straight or sitting forwards. When you do manage this though, it isn't uncommon that you hit the saddle with your pubic bone – which doesn't exactly make for a relaxed seat!

The worst of it is that due to sitting incorrectly, similar problems to those caused by a poorly fitting saddle can arise. Only by looking very carefully will you reach the right conclusions.

As an added note though, I feel I have to defend the saddler: if a horse can't relax through this back due to being ridden either roughly or by someone who is inexperienced, then his back will show the same signs of pressure that arise from a saddle that is causing problems even though they don't come from the saddle. Instead, they are due to the long muscles that lie along the back being tense and forming a type of border around where the saddle lies. In both cases the horse will arch these long muscles away, resulting in the signs described. You see this

also the stirrup leathers have to be positioned correctly. It is easier to explain this by using two riders as an example: one 165 cm tall and the other 200cm, each with their own correctly fitted saddle. If they were to swap their saddles, then the taller of the two will always fall forwards in the smaller saddle with his legs slipping back, even when the stirrups are at the correct length. A splayed seat is the result.

A saddle has to not only fit the horse, but also the rider. A tall rider will always sit splayed on a saddle that is too small...

...whilst a shorter rider in a saddle that is too large will always have to fight against legs that want to constantly slip forwards.

often caused by riders on Barock horses, especially Andalusians, whose backs and loins are especially sensitive.

And finally, I would like to say something about gel pads. If your horse has an uneven back caused, for example by scarring, lumps or similar, then a gel pad is recommended. But please do not place it directly on the horse's back, as the resulting build-up of heat and moisture can cause skin problems. You should use it with at least a cloth cover which can absorb any sweat – better still a saddle cloth or numnah between the pad and the horse's back. It can help to make a saddle whose flocking is hard feel a bit softer, although I would then ask myself whether it wouldn't be better to get the flocking made softer. Remember that when you use a gel pad you are sitting, so to speak, on jelly, and this will affect the way your horse then feels the aids through your seat. You can say goodbye to the clarity and precision of these aids.

The original cavalry curb bit is now often reproduced.

Correct bitting

Scholars argue about the choice of the correct bit. In my opinion, bits have a very secondary influence in training. I use and recommend in most cases a thin to medium loose-ring jointed snaffle, 1 to 1.5 cms wider that the horse's mouth. The new developments from the equestrian manufacturing sector that enable them to produce bits with an apple taste or using new metal alloys will not improve horsemanship. A well ridden horse will mouth, even if ridden with a rusty key as a bit.

A double bridle, using a curb bit with a bridoon, can be a very useful tool – especially with young horses. By young I mean young in their training, i.e., after backing and a basic education with a snaffle bridle.

The curb bit was developed by an African desert sheikh or rather by his blacksmith. According to legend, he was ordered to produce a bit that would allow the sheikh's horses to fly across the desert, inspiring awe and envy, as if they were riderless. The same effect that was known then, helps us today. A horse that finds it difficult to hold himself together or to shorten under a rider, may find it easier when ridden in a double bridle or curb bit, than in a snaffle. You must though not make the mistake of ignoring a horse's weaknesses, but rather use the double bridle to work on a problem with more precision.

In practice though, what happens is that a horse is ridden in a snaffle but because the horse doesn't carry himself or can't be contained, draw-reins are used to pull the horse together. I have ascertained that most riders pull too tightly on draw-reins and thus virtually throttle the last scraps of looseness or activity out of the horse. It is better to give these types of riders a double bridle and teach them how to use it properly.

Most riders have a great deal of respect for the double bridle and tend not to take such a strong hold of it. In addition a horse is more likely to rebel against a rider's hand that is too strong. Besides, a horse tends to go better in a double bridle and will not lean on the rider's hands as much, leading in turn to the rider being able to be more relaxed. In my opinion, draw-reins should be reserved for short-term use of three weeks at most, by professionals only.

'Have you, my beloved...

...ever pictured the wondrous instrument, that sits in the horse's mouth in the form of a steel rod with two arms but which also embraces his lower jaw with the help of a pretty chain? Hardly anyone gives any thought to the genius of this tool, just as we give no more thought to the wheel, pliers or roller. The curb bit is a switch that can be used to switch on so many parts of the horse's body. Used correctly, it can totally control all of the joints, but the ancient magic that slumbers in it has now been taken away. Only you may be able to wake it up.

Perhaps the curb took its first form when conjured up by mind of a noble Arab sheikh, as if in a vision, linked with the movement of his aristocratic horse. Perhaps he had it made by one of his skilful craftsmen, who could sense what was being sought. It is only the Arabs who have treated this instrument through the ages in the way that was meant when first invented; but the armoured fist of the medieval knight, charging towards his opponent on massive, armed horses relieved the invention of the elegance which was integral to its original purpose and which was supposed to be a support and help for a horse moving freely, no longer feeling the ties of gravity.

But what happened? The Arab saw, when he stepped through the door of his tent, his noble young horse, grazing loose on the desert but that came to him when he called. The horse floated towards him with raised head, filled with power, curiosity and looking for the hand that may contain a treat. He said to himself, thus can my horse move without the burden of my weight. How can I lift up this weight, what can I do for my horse so that it no longer senses this burden? So that even under my weight he continues to float when he moves? And he fell upon the idea of devising a form of support that could run along with him when in this raised and lifted posture, which made it as easy for the horse to carry his own weight when moving, as the burden of the rider on his back made it harder. It was then that he went to his craftsmen. The curb bit works because it was designed for movement that is full of impulsion and is only right for the horse that really shows impulsion in his movement. What sense is there providing support to a horse that is fixed to the spot? How pathetic the droves of today's riders look next to our Arab sheikh, reminding us of those rather uncomfortable looking equestrian monuments of less than horseman-like rulers, these riders who are rooted on the spot thoughtlessly and unfeelingly allowing the curb to work on their horse's jaw? For work it does: but since there is no impulsion for it to catch, no movement to which it gives support, it becomes a joke.'

(Quotation from Rudolf G. Bindings, 'Equestrian Hymn for my Beloved' published by Olms Verlag, Hildesheim).

Balance before movement, not the other way round

The most frequent problem that a rider has to struggle with is getting a good contact through the reins without losing the lightness through the poll or the quality of the movement. The cause for this is often mistaken: it doesn't always lie with the flexibility or suppleness of the horse but rather often with a lack of balance. You might think it is a case of 'no suppleness, no balance' but on the contrary, it is more a lack of balance that leads to a horse getting tense.

Because riders are often impatient and want to try to advance their horse's training too quickly, then horses will often lack the strength required if they are going to develop balance. Building up muscles requires far more time than the training of certain movements or exercises. Problems with balance may also arise, as mentioned before, if the horse is ridden above-tempo, i.e. too quickly, because a rider wrongly interprets what is meant by riding 'forwards'.

> The right speed creates the right rhythm and helps in establishing the contact.

How do you create expression?

Expressive movement comes primarily from the impulsion created through the hindquarters together with the horse's relaxedness and balance. The German term 'Losgelassenheit' is a term that is difficult to translate with one word, and means a combination of relaxation, suppleness and looseness. Here we will use the word 'relaxedness'.

If you were to try to create expression from a horse's speed then you will put the contact at risk, since a horse will try to lift up out of the contact in order to readjust his balance to counter the rider's

This Friesian's passage shows a perfect combination of impulsion, power and balance.

Correct: after riding passage, the horse is ridden down into a lower outline.

In a good, forwards trot the horse is stepping through and covering more ground.

effect. If the rider prevents this then the horse will get stressed, tense up, and will start to run in an attempt to find his balance.

We are constantly talking about developing impulsion, rhythm and relaxedness, but often forget that balance is the most important prerequisite for all of these. Balance is also the most important prerequisite for the development of collection, although here it is vital to keep the rider's balance at the front of your mind. In collection the horse has to work with a degree of tautness throughout its body, but must not actually be tense. The rider often makes exactly this mistake: he tenses up because he wants to create this physical tautness. Ideally, though, the rider should only have to ensure that he is perfectly balanced and remain relaxed in himself. In doing this he becomes more predictable for the horse and as a result the horse is better able to balance both itself and its rider.

The seal and the ball

It is precisely this ability to rebalance that is a huge problem for us now, working as so many of us do in offices. If a horse becomes unbalanced, riders say that they have to compensate with huge rocking counter-er movements or, even worse, they wave their hands and reins around as if they were tightrope walkers. And so along comes my comparison of a seal in the circus with his ball: if the ball was alive and tried to help the seal balance itself, the seal would have a nervous breakdown in every second performance. The seal makes balancing the ball look so easy because the ball is perfectly round and predictable and hasn't come alive.

I see this again and again in riding: if I am trying to put a rider right, I will ask him just to concentrate on balancing himself and not pay any attention to the horse's movement, just letting himself be carried. As if by magic the horse will immediately develop more quality in the pace, more looseness and, above all, improved balance. If this result can be secured with daily training and you would then like to get more out of the movement, then you only need to apply your aids carefully to assist the horse.

The significance of the seat

The seat is central to any discussion of riding and training. As a trainer I have my own opinion: a rider can only alter his seat when he has pointers. By this I mean that the horse must react to any change and the rider needs feedback from his horse. The horse is the best teacher when it comes to the seat. My role as a trainer is to be the moderator, helping the rider to correct himself by using the feeling he is getting from the horse.

The rider should be like a puppet with strings attached to the head, chin, breastbone, hand and toes, sitting tilted slightly forwards on the horse in order for his weight to be evenly spread on the saddle and into the stirrups. In other words, he is suspended over the horse.

This slight inclination forwards is important so that the rider doesn't sit into the horse's back and the horse is better able to swing through more easily. At the same time this also prevents the rider falling backwards when the horse quickens, and instead is straightened up by this increase in pace.

The rider should always sit on the deepest part of the saddle – but it is significant how he does this. In the zero position a rider will be sitting on his seatbones. He will be very unstable, easily tipping either forwards or backwards. In order to be more stable he has to use the pubic bone as the third point of balance, although no real pressure is taken up from the seat. Using the three-point position, a woman would probably find it uncomfortable and for a man it is also not pleasant.

It is the trainer's role to support the rider so that she can correct her seat by herself.

Helpful cords

Correcting the seat is often difficult – for the person being corrected as well as the trainer doing the correcting. A rider needs all his energy to change something and the instructions given by his trainer may bounce off him since he either doesn't hear them or doesn't understand them. This is unsatisfactory on both sides. Added to this is that while he might get it right during a lesson, at home he will revert back to old habits. As a result I began to develop and look for training aids at an early stage to first of all help to achieve results during training sessions, and then started looking for things that could help riders when they were back at home.

Amongst my favourites are Thera-Band®, developed for use by physiotherapists. They are easy to use yet very effective. They are usually sold as a set containing a red and a blue stretchy cord. The red is less strong and is stretched diagonally from the rider's lower shoulder to

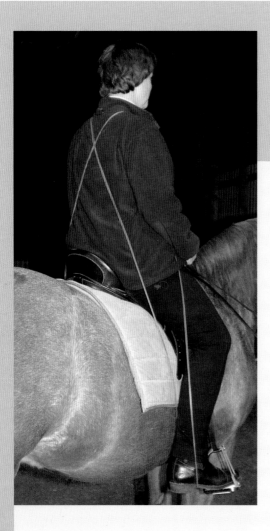

leg is lifted up and the rider feels as if he is losing his stirrups – resulting in him stretching his legs longer and looser.

As a result of these stretchy cords, even the most tense of riders will begin to relax their body and move with the horse, sitting much straighter than before. These cords have another advantage. Where a rider tends to grip with his legs, I shorten the cords a bit so that he needs to use more strength to make his legs longer. It is almost physically impossible to stretch your legs while at the same time gripping with them. The result is astonishing – horses that are tense or aren't going forwards suddenly move much more freely and more forwards. In addition, these cords can help to correct problems with the contact, since if the horse's shoulder is being squeezed by the legs then the withers cannot open completely and the horse can't move freely over their back. This is seen most often with Barock horses (by this I refer particularly to the Iberian breeds such as Andalusians and Lusitanos) because they have more shoulder movement than, for example, warmbloods.

loop under the heel on the opposite side with enough tension so that it is only just comfortable for the rider. The blue cord, which is stronger, is looped from the higher shoulder across to the opposite heel. Thanks to the pressure on both shoulders the rider is automatically straightened through his whole body from shoulder to heel. As a result of the pressure on the soles of the feet, the

Turning your body

The turning of the body plays a significant role in riding and is often underestimated. To give you an example: a beginner wants to turn in on a circle but the horse runs through his shoulder to the outside back onto the outside track. Let's assume that the rider has correctly turned his shoulders so that they are in line with the horse's shoulders and he has sat in the direction of the movement – despite this, the horse hasn't turned off the track.

What has gone wrong? There is a difference between pulling the inside shoulder back and moving the outside shoulder forwards. The secret lies in the fact that the human body feels totally different if you take your inside shoulder back, as in doing so you will use primarily the muscles in your back. If on the other hand you push your outside shoulder forwards, you will be using the muscles in your chest and stomach more.

If a riding instructor doesn't bother practising this with his students, so that this difference can be distinguished and used appropriately, then it will often, to stay with our initial example, be the case that the rider pulls on the inside rein and subsequently pulls his inside shoulder back. Instead it would be better to allow his outside shoulder to be pulled forwards through the outside rein into the turn.

In classical dressage it is said that in a volte (10m circle) the rider should sit to the outside whilst at the same time always sitting straight. This seems contradictory but this isn't the case at all. When a horse bends through his body the saddle's outside panel is lifted up higher than the inside one so that a rider sitting square and straight in the saddle will feel more pressure through his outside seat bone. If a horse tries to run through his outside shoulder and the rider collapses even slightly through his inside hip, then this pressure is intensified.

To ride on to a circle it is important to move your outside shoulder forwards – this uses totally different muscles than if you were to pull your inside shoulder back.

When bending, the outside half of the horse's back will be raised higher so that the rider may feel that he has to sit to the inside, which is incorrect. In classical dressage the rider should always sit to the outside when riding on a small circle. The reason for this is that if the rider sits square then he will feel more pressure through the outside seat bone precisely because in the bend the horse's back will lift up to the outside.

In half-pass, the rider's straight and open upper body leans in the direction of the movement, without collapsing through his hip.

If the pace is too fast, the hindleg will remain on the ground for too long, placing too much strain on the horse's loins.

Sitting in the direction of the movement

Referring back to the previous comments, many will now point out that you should be sitting in the direction of the movement so that the horse can step through underneath himself. This is correct, however first of all the horse has to himself be going in the direction of the movement so that the rider can be sitting in the same direction too.

Let's take the half-pass as an example. When I start to work on the half-pass, I sit to the outside from time to time to prevent the horse, when the bend and flexion is correct, from crossing over to the wrong side, i.e. through the outside shoulder. Once the horse is moving in the right direction, I will put more weight down through my inside stirrup so that the horse steps more energetically forwards and sideways into the half-pass. To correct a half-pass you don't lean down to the outside, but instead you would pull your outside shoulder back.

The rider can then stay sitting square and yet still ride from the outside to the inside. At the same time this turning of the shoulder lifts the inside hip, opening the door wide to the inside for the horse.

Finding the right tempo at the right time

Today there is all too often the misconception that a horse can be warmed up properly by chasing him around the school, either on the lunge or under saddle.

At first glance it may even seem that the horse is more expressive due to the faster pace. This impression though doesn't come as a result of balance or impulsion from behind though, but rather out of fear and above all from the centrifugal force created by his hooves. A horse that is ridden at too fast a pace cannot step through under his centre of gravity, and instead takes many more shorter steps with his quarters trailing. In addition, the quarters – as already described in the previous chapter – will remain in contact with the ground for too long. If, for example, you worked your horse in trot from his fastest to slowest pace and then went back to his fastest, then the rider would feel when he had the best movement from the horse and when the horse was best able to carry him with him. This moment is the right tempo at the right time. If you did the same test when lungeing, then you would see that at a particular tempo the horse will go round and look comfortable within itself. When lungeing though, the ideal speed is often faster that that when being ridden since the horse can move without the additional weight of the rider.

In the case of older horses, their tempo can change according to the weather. When it is cold and wet they will often be slower; when warm and dry they will be faster. In the case of warming up in particular, in addition to the correct rein, the correct tempo plays as important a role. As you continue to train your horse you will be asking him to go more forwards, but you should always ensure that the good feeling you got at the right tempo when warming up is taken with you and maintained, and not lost. There are, however, many horses that are very laid back, never mind just too comfortable or even dozy. It is totally legitimate to wake these types of horses up by asking for sudden increases then decreases of pace, from time to time. Mostly though, horses that appear to be lazy when starting to work are actually just very tense. If you try to ride these horses forwards too quickly, without warming them up

properly, then they will only get tenser. Here too it is a case of observing them very carefully.

If, for example, you were to visit a martial arts school, you would see that those movements that are later carried out extremely quickly are initially perfected by doing them in slow motion in order to keep the muscles loose and relaxed. This is incidentally extremely strenuous and draining and serves to build up not only muscles but also condition.

In the case of horses, there are two other factors that need to be considered. First of all, as an animal of flight, they are very sensitive to external optical and acoustic stimuli. By using slower movements the horse can be made to concentrate more on both itself and its rider. Secondly, the hindquarters, in contrast to the forehand, cannot necessarily go ever slower indefinitely. This means that if you ask a horse to go at a tempo that is slower than the hindquarters can actually move, then the horse will get shorter and the hindquarters will be moving increasingly clearer and more effectively. By using this increased degree of effectiveness in the movement, you can ride more forwards as long as the feeling of harmony and lightness remains, looking not only for the right tempo but also for the right shape.

If you take the time to think, from the perspective of biomechanics, about how a horse is contained, then riding is nothing other than the application of pure biomechanics. In the ideal, a horse moves from back to front. The hindquarters step under the rider's weight and the body pushes through forwards and upwards. Just as is the case with the hindquarters, so it is with his head and neck: the weaker the muscles in the horse's torso are, then the lower I need to position the horse's head and neck so that the withers remain open and the hindquarters can work effectively.

A rider's most important goal: harmony in movement in whatever he does.

Strengthening work on the **lunge**

The horses with which this chapter deals suffer from problems with their musculature. They may have weak flexor muscles, especially in the abdomen and the torso, or the muscles in the back and pelvis are so tense that the horse has no chance of being able to collect and come underneath itself. In both cases, the horse is not in a position to be able to carry additional weight and if it did, it would only create greater and longer term problems. If you were to ride such a horse it would only make the training process longer and more difficult. It is true that certain muscles groups can really only be worked on when the horse is ridden, but the training of certain muscle mechanics and relaxing of tense areas is just so much easier without the burden of additional weight.

Working with the gymnastic training rein

Most normal types of side-reins or training aids have one problem – they don't allow the horse to find a 'relief position' or take up an outline that is most comfortable for him, in other words they are restricting and above all else they are inflexible. A horse takes up such a relief position to give certain parts of his body a break, in other words in order to relax them. If a training aid doesn't allow this, then the horse may go in the required outline, but certainly not relaxed and loose. Other training aids on the other hand are so flexible, that the horse doesn't look for and take up the contact but runs through it instead.

The 'breaking point' of the gymnastic rein: in an emergency this clip will snap to protect the horse's mouth. (Photo: Stroscher)

I developed this gymnastic rein myself several years ago to enable me to be able to more effectively work with horses that were either very tense or had very sensitive mouths. It helps to make tense horses more relaxed and younger horses to build up their muscle development. Since it allows the horse's head total freedom of movement it is especially suitable for horses that are being treated for skeletal problems and parallel to this are being worked to loosen and build up their muscles. It allows these types of horses to take up the previously mentioned relief position or outline – such as those who tilt their head or turn their head to the outside on a circle – and doesn't tie them down into a certain shape. This type of rein also helps young horses to find their own balance more quickly.

When it comes to safety, the gymnastic rein sets new standards. The single length of rein is fastened on both ends to either side of the surcingle with a plastic clip that will snap in an emergency.

If the horse is frightened and jumps into the rein or throws its head up suddenly, the clip will break, thereby protecting the horse's mouth. The hook is quick and easy to replace before continuing with work. It is of course always important to ensure that the rein's length is appropriate for the stage of the horse's training.

When using the rein for the first time on the lunge you should, as when using running reins, attach them to the surcingle between the front legs, take them up through the bit and then attach them back to the surcingle on his side so they are parallel to the ground to allow the horse to get used to them. Adjust the rein so that the horse is put on a light contact but remember that the horse has to get used to it and trust it before you should gradually shorten it even more. Begin work at a walk, warming the

To allow the horse to get used to the gymnastic rein as well as when warming up, it should be attached like a running rein.

horse up firstly on his better side before proceeding to trot. The more a horse can warm up and relax, the more you can shorten the rein until his nose is on the vertical, or rather tending to be slightly behind it. You should be able to draw a horizontal line from the withers to the poll, with the neck forming a gently curving bridge between them.

The horse's hollow side

Every horse is naturally one sided. Just as we are born right or left handed, finding it easier to use one hand over the other, so a horse has a 'good' and a 'bad' side. We can also describe this as being hollow on one side, linked to the different length of muscles on each side. It is often maintained that this comes from the way the foetus lies in the mare. I don't believe this though, since in Iceland for example most horses are hollow to the right – there the horses are handled more from the right than the left and are also mounted from the right. This means that the muscles on this, the right side, are shorter while those on the other side have a greater ability to stretch. In Germany and England, where

As the horse begins to work properly, the gymnastic rein should be placing pressure on the bit from above, providing the same effect as riding with a raised inside hand.

horses are usually handled from the left side, most horses are left handed, or hollow to the left. You can recognise which is the hollow side usually by the fact that the mane will fall on this side. One of the principle aims of schooling for dressage is to straighten the horse during its basic training. The shorter muscles on the one side should be worked on so they gradually become able to be stretched just as well as the muscles on the other side.

This type of device is best suited for horses that need to be encouraged to stretch over their back and work forwards into a longer and lower outline. It is important that you don't try and get them to drop their head and neck, which this type of work is trying to achieve, by tying them down into this outline.

Once you have worked your horse thoroughly with the gymnastic reins in its initial position – allowing at least three or four weeks, you can start to work using the second variation for lungeing. To do this you attach the headpiece that comes with the reins into the horse's bridle or cavesson. At the start of the session, warm the horse up as you have done so far, with the usual length of rein. After the warm up, connect the part of the rein that runs between the poll and the surcingle, to the headpiece. As a result, the rein will be shortened and will also give the same effect as if riding with a raised hand. The bit will receive pressure from above, causing the horse to open his mouth, flex through the poll and begin to mouth on the bit. He will work with a slightly lowered poll and more bend over the neck, causing him to round up his back. This stretches the back muscles and, at the same time, the withers will be pulled up and forwards as a result of the increased tension through the nuchal ligaments. This enables the quarters and the abdominal muscles to work more effectively and strengthen.

At the end of the session, when cooling down at walk, you should detach the rein from the headpiece and allow him to stretch down for a few minutes.

When working your horse on the lunge like this, you should always ensure that the horse moves quietly and rhythmically forwards – working hard but not becoming too rushed. Begin by lungeing for no more than 20 minutes at first and increase this as the horse's fitness and concentration span grows.

Only begin with the trot work once the horse is relaxed and warmed up in walk. Even muscle development will more likely occur from walk than trot. Later it is useful to work in canter to further build up the abdominal muscles. The trot, on the other hand, will improve the horse's relaxedness, suppleness and rhythm as well as his fitness.

Through the appropriate use of the gymnastic rein when lungeing, you will quickly see a positive change in your horse. But remember – this training aid is not a cure-all. Should you see no improvement, then I would recommend that your horse sees an equine physiotherapist or that you have your veterinary surgeon examine him.

When working on the lunge, the horse should always be straight – meaning that quarters, forehand and poll should always be in a straight line, even on a circle: When jumping, riders will get young horses to approach jumps out of a circle because this steadies the horse and helps the horse to keep to the right line without the riders constantly having to interfere with its way of going. It is just the same when lungeing: if you 'spin' your horse around on a circle so that his head, neck and body is not in a line and may swing out away from the lunge, then the horse can neither relax nor be balanced. The horse's body can only become more stable and steady when the impulsion from the quarters goes in a straight line over the back into the forehand and poll and through into the rein.

The horse needs to carefully be accustomed to the use of a whip as an extension of your arm. (Photo: Stroscher)

The whip and its effect

There is a huge variety and quantity of lunge whips on the market today. Very few of these though are of the quality required to school a horse properly in-hand. A whip that is suitable for in-hand work needs to be both light and flexible. Best suited are those made from fibreglass or cane with a leather thong and a tip made from nylon. Nylon used for the end of a whip has the advantage of being able to produce a good noise when needed, without having to overuse the leather thong itself, and can be easily replaced when necessary. The length of the whip used will depend on the type of work you are doing. When working on a lunge on the typical 20 metre circle, the body of the whip should be 1.6m in length, and the thong 3.5m. The relationship between the length of the whip and the thong is important for it to be easy to handle. Rule of thumb is usually for there to be a ratio of 1:2 between the length of the whip and the thong.

The same applies whether on the lunge or being ridden: the walk and trot will help the horse to loosen and relax; the canter will build him up.

The whip extends your hand's reach. It is not there to punish or hit the horse, but instead should solely be used to make the wishes of the person lungeing clear. This won't work, of course, if the horse is scared of the whip. For this reason it is important to do some basic exercises to build trust before beginning to start lungeing. Start by stroking the horse softly with the lungeing whip until he allows himself to be touched all over and perceives being stroked with this aid as a reward.

The whip thus serves to refine the aids and has the same role as spurs do when riding. The horse should neither fear being touched by the whip nor be frightened by the noise is creates. You should, without any fuss, get your horse used to the noise a whip can make. Always combine the use of the whip with a voice command. You don't after all want to startle your horse, but rather just create forward momentum. The whip should trigger a reaction and show a horse how, when and where he should use which muscles.

• For an improvement in the quality of the walk you should touch the whip to the base of the tail and the quarters from above and behind.

• To improve the trot, you will need to flick the whip behind the quarters at the height of the horse's hocks from behind and below.

• When a half-halt isn't enough to move the horse into canter, then touching the whip just behind the elbow should achieve the required results.

• In general, you can get a horse to collect or contain himself by touching the whip to the large plate of tendons located under his tummy which will cause him to lift and round his back.

Whoever thinks that you get better results by using a whip with more force is barking up the wrong tree – the horse will lose his trust in the whip and will just tense and take off.

It's hard to believe: as a result of correct training, even a Friesian can go quietly in a forwards canter.

The basic paces

The walk

When lungeing, as is the case whenever you are working with your horse, you should also begin in walk. Apart from the fact that, like every human athlete, the horse too needs about 25 minutes to warm up – the joint cartilage in particular needs this 'running in' time so that they can fulfil their shock absorbing function – the slower pace gives the person lungeing time to give the rider instructions and the horse the chance to think and react accordingly.

For horses that have not built up their muscles, it can be a good idea to add in one or two sessions of walk totalling up to 60 minutes (for example on a horse walker) in addition to the training sessions.

The more regular the walk is in these sessions, the more valuable it is for building up the muscles. In addition, the rhythm of the walk – contrary to the general opinion of many dressage trainers – is less liable to interference. Often gaited horses such as (Icelandic ponies or Tennessee walking horses) and horses, that have been worked for too long with too much hand, tend towards a pace-like walk. Instead of walking with a clear four-beat rhythm they walk with the foreleg and hindleg on the same side hitting the ground almost at the same time. This is usually the result of stress, tension and being too hectic. Pacing occurs when the horse's back is so tense that he doesn't

A good walk is worth its weight in gold – it is difficult to improve it by training.

move it: as a result though of the ability of the spinal column to move like a snake in a wavy motion, the pace can revert back to walk. Usually you don't have to do anything specific since the problem will often sort itself out on the lunge.

The walk – by which we mean the natural walk, when the horse moves relaxed and happy in his steps – is however the one gait that is least likely to be improved by training. In the case of the majority of horses that I have trained, the walk was often worsened by the wrong work being done either when ridden or on the lunge and improved gradually during the course of my training.

> The walk is well suited to building up specific groups of muscles, thus balancing out any unevenness in the musculature.

The trot

The trot, in comparison to the walk, is more dynamic and can more easily be changed. It is in this gait that both balance and collection can be worked on. In addition, it promotes a better basic condition and has a loosening effect, because in the trot the back swings regularly up and down. As a result of the diagonal footfall in a two-beat rhythm, the way the horse has been created means that its head and neck are kept still, which later helps in establishing a contact. The trot is therefore the basic pace used in the course of every dressage education when it comes to training and working through exercises. In terms of building up muscles, the trot isn't so relevant, since the loading placed on the muscles by the regular swinging between the extensor and flexor muscles is relatively limited. For the horse, the trot is the gait in which he expends the least energy!

As a result of the regular rhythm of the trot, it is the pace in which it is easiest to loosen and warm the horse up.

The canter

The canter is a three-beat jumping gait. The transition to canter is for most horses not as easy as the transition to trot, since cantering quietly in a confined area demands a certain amount of balance and strength. Gaited horses and those that are a bit weak are those that tend towards having a four-beat canter, especially on the lunge. Otherwise, they may tend to take off. In both cases you should avoid the canter when lungeing, at least until the horse is more secure in both walk and trot. This is especially the case when you don't have an ideal surface or good ground conditions and there is a danger that the horse may slip. In such poor conditions you would destroy the trust that you have taken so much time to build up.

In the two-beat rhythm of the trot, the back swings evenly up and down.

The canter is characterized by a clear, jumping movement.

In the walk you are suppling the horse for the trot, then the trot loosens and collects the horse in preparation for the canter. In the canter you are able to build up and improve the horse's musculature needed for riding.

It is important when moving from trot into canter that you don't allow your horse to run into the new gait. Don't let your horse trot faster and faster until he canters out of desperation, but rather make your aids obvious and clear so they act like a key

turning the ignition. When starting out, ask the horse for a quiet trot or even walk and give a clear voice command, such as 'And canter' together with the whip used just behind his elbow to drive him on. At the same time give a clear tug on the lunge line. This will cause the horse to spring more energetically forwards with both its inside fore and hindlegs in order to try and counteract this 'interference', especially later when the horse may be wearing side reins. In 90 per cent of cases this will result in one or two canter strides. By asking for the canter transition in this way, you will achieve a good quality working canter, especially when practiced frequently to secure it. As a rule of thumb, the canter should be a touch slower that the trot out of which it came as only this type of canter will have a positive effect on the musculature.

By getting a correct transition to canter on the lunge, you are preparing the horse in the best way for the leg and rein aids that will be used later for the transition when ridden. At the same time the danger that the horse will strike off on the wrong leg is relatively small. Should your horse go disunited in the canter, either at strike off or during a canter phase, then this is a sign of a lack of balance, or that the horse has been pulled off balance by the lunge line. In this case either the trot before the transition was too slow or you were asking for the canter too soon.

To begin with, your horse will try and balance himself when cantering on the lunge by turning his head and neck to the outside. This is a sign that he is lacking suppleness, but this will change following further work in trot. This is why you should simply tolerate your horse turning its head to the outside: under no circumstances try to 'correct' it with unforgiving side-reins or similar. By doing this you would risk causing painful tension in the neck muscles as the horse needs his neck as a balancing pole.

If you have invested patience and have been consistent in the preparatory work for the canter, then this will reward you with an expected quality of canter and will improve and hasten the development of the horse's muscles. In my opinion so many horses have problems with their balance and stability because in comparison to the amount of trot, they do too little quiet and regular canter. I have sometimes (rather sarcastically) been known to say, 'this horse will be loosened up in rising trot, until it loosens itself.'

Cavaletti work

Lungeing doesn't just train the horse's body, but also its mind. Cavaletti work especially helps to establish his inner strength – it helps timid horses to become braver, and in addition helps to build condition. You often see nervous and fearful horses blossom following this type of work, as they become more and more self-confident. A healthy mind and body is just as important for a horse.

A horse that still has problems with cavalettis should not be backed. Body and mind are not as yet sufficiently developed. Only when he can carry out the work over cavalettis in a bridle, surcingle and side-reins is he ready for backing.

You can start cavaletti work as soon as the horse has mastered the basics of lungeing. First of all just place a single cavaletti across the track and ask the horse to go over it in walk and trot. If the horse shies the first time and runs out, get a helper to lead him over the pole the first few times until he loses his fear. If the horse goes calmly over a single pole without losing rhythm then add another, then another, so he is going over three cavalettis. Pay attention that the distances are set for the horse's stride as only then will he be able to step over the poles whilst maintaining a clean rhythm. Otherwise you are putting him in front of an impossible task that is more likely to destroy trust than build self confidence.

Working over cavalettis on the lunge has innumerable benefits for your horse's suppleness and has a positive effect on the horse's mental state.

In order to determine what the correct distance is for the horse, lay out a fan of poles with an inside distance of 80 cm and outer distance of 150 cm between the poles. Then lunge your horse over the fan in trot on a looser line so that he can chose what is the most comfortable distance for him. Note this distance for the future when setting up the cavalettis.

In a more advanced stage of training, you can use the cavaletti to improve the horse's length of stride. At this stage though it would be too much for a young horse. At this point of his training the cavalleti should only be used to encourage the horse to lift his legs a bit higher, leading him to swing more through his back and become more relaxed. The horse's impulsion and expression improves when trotting over cavaletti, which in turn is good for his suppleness.

Working over cavaletti does so much more: it not only improves impulsion and rhythm, but also teaches a horse awareness of his own body, especially the co-ordination between his eyes and feet. A horse that has learned to look where he steps is later on much steadier on his feet when hacking out.

As soon as the horse can canter safely and quietly on the lunge, you can work over the cavaletti in this gait as well. To do this set out at least five cavaletti as if for trot work, and then take out the second and fourth cavaletti. This will then create the correct distance to be able to go over them in a quiet and collected canter, and in the longer term improve the canter work. In the case of horses that do not or cannot canter well, this will help them on the way to improvement.

Cane cavaletti

Cavalettis made out of rattan or cane are particularly useful. They are light and easy to move around and also extremely bendy! If a horse steps on a cane pole, it will give and spring back. The danger of the horse injuring himself on heavy cavaletti is thus avoided from the start. Horses work well with cane cavaletti as they register the impact from the vibration through the cane. In addition, cane cavaletti tend to be lower than those made from solid wood and so the risk of hooking the lunge line around the cavaletti is also reduced.

More on the theme of in-hand work can be found in my book 'The long-reining handbook,' also published by Cadmos.

Moving from **lungeing** to ridden work

When you start to ride your horse (again) after the basic lunge work, it is important to wind back your own expectations and demands and to start to build your work up again, likely starting at a level that is beneath the level you were working at on the lunge.

What does riding mean?
- Moving as one.
- A relaxed interaction between horse and rider.
- Guiding your horse, not mastering him.
- Steering involves moving your balance by sitting in the direction of the desired movement.

A horse's character and conformation will determine what the right approach to his training is.
Whether it's a Friesian with a long back,...

...a warmblood...

...or an Andalusian. As can be seen here, a horse going round and deep has nothing to do with the infamous 'Rollkur'. These horses are relaxed and happy, because the deeper outline helps them to work through their back.

How do I work different horses?

The way I start out a training session will make a difference to its success. It depends fundamentally on knowing what I want to achieve and work on, which then influences the way I warm up my horse.

Here is an example. If I am faced with a highly strung or excited horse with which I am planning to work on improving his piaffe and passage, then I would begin with a quiet but energetic warm up. With a heavier and quieter type I would more likely choose a warm up that saved his energy but was slightly more exciting. I just can't understand why there are so many instructors and trainers out there that neither structure nor supervise their pupil's warm-up. A horse has to be in the right mood – one that is focused on his training! That is more important than supervising the training session that follows.

Every rider, regardless of ability, knows that if you are feeling happy and satisfied then you will be more relaxed in your riding and likely to achieve more. On the other hand, on days when you aren't in such a good mood, then it is often difficult to do anything right. If you simply aren't in the mood, why should your horse be any different?

One of the most frequent problems that riders have with their horses is working to achieve and maintain a steady contact through the reins. At the same time, almost every trainer and rider has their own secret recipe for this. Once you start to examine these more closely you discover that

Every rider knows that being in a good mood when training has a huge impact on the result.

each recipe is slightly different and that every rider prefers a certain type of horse that is often characterised by specific strengths and weaknesses, so that it is possible to train all of these horses using the same techniques. What this means is that there are many different ways and options of establishing and maintaining contact. What is much more important though, is that not every horse that is either beginning his training or perhaps is in a phase of retraining, will improve by concentrating totally upon the contact.

If you were to throw all breeds of horses into a pot and then sort them out not by their origin, but instead by the strengths and weaknesses that are significant for our training of them, then we would put them into two large groups. The first group would consist of horses that are rectangular in shape: their strengths lie in being able to move fluidly and energetically forwards, their paces being well suited to extension, but they will likely have problems with collection. In this group, contact is usually established by working on circles of various sizes, consistently asking the horse to work into the outside rein in walk and trot. If you lift the inside hand when doing this sort of work then the horse will be easier to

It is especially important with sensitive horses to work quietly, so that the horse is relaxed – this being the most important prerequisite for collection, which will come later.

work through and will give more easily through his poll. With this sort of horse the use of stronger aids, especially with the hand, is often counter productive. The quality of movement, motivation and above all the horse's looseness and relaxedness will all suffer, since with their natural forwardness the head and neck act like the balancing pole used by a high wire walker. Without this pole both the wire walker and the horse will panic and have real problems.

The second large group consists of horses whose strength is collection: they are more likely to have a square conformation and are often more uphill in their outline, with a raised forehand. Most horses of this type are either of Iberian origin or warmblood horses refined with English thoroughbred or Arab blood. When training these horses you should keep two things in mind: on the one hand, they are more prone to muscle tension, and on the other hand, they tend to be more highly strung – meaning their temperament might sometimes stand in your way. Here it is a case of getting both body and mind to simultaneously concentrate and relax. Riding them forwards or warming them up using transitions would be wrong for these types at the start of their work and would only serve to make them more nervous.

Trainers faced with rectangular shaped representatives of the second group will have even more difficulty. In addition to having to cope with a more highly-strung animal, the trainer is also faced with one that will likely have poor musculature through the shoulder and abdomen. As a result the horse will tend to hollow its back, trail its quarters and poke its breastbone forwards and down. It will feel like you are riding a runaway railway sleeper! In short, these are horses with a raised forehand and a certain gift for collection, but with a poor canter. This is often found in Arabs and Friesians. Friesians in particular have gone in the opposite direction to thoroughbreds: whilst the warmblood has been refined by crossing it with the thoroughbred, the Friesian was originally a horse with a thoroughbred stamp that was crossed with heavier breeds in order to suit the new demands of the nineteenth century, for example from agriculture, but also to make it more suitable for human consumption. It is only more recently that the Dutch Friesian Breed society has changed course so that the Friesian is now being bred more in line with its original direction as a lighter and more elegant riding horse.

If you are training a youngster of this type, then you should gradually and quietly build up the work on the lunge so that you can then continue this work at a relaxed walk when in the saddle. When training or correcting older horses from this last group it is wise to work through a lungeing programme that initially relaxes and then helps to collect the horse, before starting with ridden work. Even then every session should start with a period of walk on a good contact. Horses of this type should be ridden clearly under tempo and use voltes, circles and other bending exercises to improve their concentration. Of course this means not hanging onto the reins, but rather riding the horse from the leg into the hand. This might at first

sound contradictory, since when faced with a horse with a hurried walk you tend not to think of using your legs but rather of holding it back. Remember the rule: I will only get a quiet canter when it has come from a quiet and regular trot, and in order to get a quiet trot, I need a quiet walk – whereby 'quiet' means both slightly collected and well balanced.

If I want a quiet walk, then metaphorically speaking, I need to ride the halt forwards. After about ten or fifteen minutes in walk on a long rein, start your training session by working from halt to walk, riding the walk step by step forwards. When doing this you should, at any time, be in a position to be able to halt by simply ceasing to ride forwards (i.e. by stopping to use your legs or seat) and not by pulling on the reins. The constant effect of your legs will help to stimulate the abdominal muscles and the back will begin to round up, and the horse will begin to concentrate on the softest of aids and so mentally will also relax. You can make it easier for the horse by varying the tempo, although you should never chose a tempo that feels rushed. The aim should be for the horse to be soft in the hand and mouthing on the bit, relaxed, contained and eventually on a stable contact so that the transition into a quiet trot is possible.

Relax and breathe

It may sound absurd, but it is true: of course horses breathe, otherwise they couldn't move. When being ridden though, many horses hold their breath for short periods of time or strain to breathe. Relaxed breathing will often start with a soft and rhythmical grunting or groaning and ends with single or multiple snorting or blowing out through the nostrils. If you are riding outside then you should be able to tell from the rhythmical snorting and breathing what pace the horse is in. Rhythm and breathing as well as balance are indispensable tools for the warming up and suppling of a horse. The key to a supple horse consists of riding him first of all on his hollow side (on the rein that he bends more easily to) in both walk and trot with a bend appropriate to his level of training. The time you should spend riding him on this rein before changing direction is decided by how large the difference is between the two reins. The greater the difference, the more one-sided the horse. It is especially important to watch that the tempo is not too fast. The tempo should be less than the usual working pace, and the more tense or stiffer the horse, then the slower the work should begin. The rhythm should be increased when the horse feels as if he is working round and is easily contained – this may be the case before others can see this in him. If you ride too forwards too early, the horse will set himself against the rider again because he can no longer work through his entire body and will lose balance. The horse may be desperately maintaining his outline and look good, but doesn't feel good any longer. The aim of work to supple the horse is to achieve regular breathing. This will only happen when the tempo, rhythm, balance and attitude are all in harmony.

Freeing up the back

One of the first goals of any rider is to ride the horse on the bit. Often a rider gives no thought as to why at the beginning of a session the horse doesn't work easily on the bit. An attempt will be made using a variety of techniques to establish a contact. In the case of horses kept stabled, their backs are more prone to tension due to the long periods of time standing in one place and so, as a rider, I have to address this issue first. The most effective way to stretch the back is to create in the horse the desire to do this for himself.

To do this, the back muscles are put under stress by shortening the reins together with an increasingly active leg. The reins should be shortened inch by inch, preceded each time by the leg until you can't get any shorter.

Keep like this for a short while, until the horse indicates that he is feeling a bit too constrained. Then ride the horse, again inch by inch and by using the leg before letting the rein out, into a deeper and lower outline. As soon as the rein is so long that I can no longer drive him into a contact with my legs, I take the rein up again, but inch by inch ensuring that the leg aid always comes before the hand. You will feel every time you shorten and lengthen how the horse becomes looser and relaxes – a state that is always worth striving for.

It is important when doing this exercise that you literally really do move inch by inch and not take up or release the reins all at once, in order to ensure that you always have the horse on the aids and that he doesn't run up against the reins.

In order to free the back, the reins are shortened bit by bit until the horse shows that it is getting uncomfortable for him.

You then let the horse stretch and take the rein down.

The longer the back in relation to the neck is, the deeper a horse can be ridden.

Using the leg to ask the horse to give through his poll

When a horse has reached a more advanced level of training and is supple, then you can begin to practice an opposing exercise, in order to encourage the horse to work deeper and through his neck.

First variation

At halt, use your legs softly, slowly and both at the same time to drive the horse into your hand. Your hands should maintain a firm but flexible contact. If the horse begins to mouth on the bit then you are doing it right. The mouthing will relax the poll and the horse will take up a soft contact. The mouthing is caused by the pressure caused by your legs through the abdominal muscles which in turn lift the back. The horse begins to square up, the wither opens and the neck and poll are lightened.

After this, ride a few yards in walk, halt and repeat the exercise. If you can achieve a good contact using your legs in halt, then move onto trying to achieve the same in walk. If you don't manage it, then halt again, repeat at halt and then move back into walk. Only when you can get it in walk should you proceed in trot. Behind this exercise is the thought that the horse connects working through his neck and poll with the soft pressure through the legs. In addition you are communicating through your legs in every lesson, ensuring that the horse halts square and is carrying himself.

Why is it necessary at all to encourage a rectangular shaped horse with a high set on neck, and thus a higher head carriage, to accept the contact and then move off forwards? If we look at the horse's anatomy again, the withers and its neural spine are at the centre of a horse's movement. The horse's body makes every effort to keep the vertebra apart, as if the wither was being fanned out upwards. This can occur in two ways: either via the croup muscles that relax as the horse steps through and underneath itself, at the same time pulling the withers up and back, or through the nuchal ligament that connects the withers with the neck.

In our training this means that if we were to ride the horse forwards then the muscles in the quarters would be responsible for the forwards 'push' as well as keeping the withers open at the same time. This double strain usually leads to the hindquarter muscles getting tired more quickly, which in turn makes it more difficult to strengthen and build up the muscles. Even the supposedly easy to ride Barock horses have weak loins that can't transmit the strength of the hindquarters through to the rest of the body, with the result that you virtually have two horses in one. The cause of irregular paces can often be traced to the loins and can develop into lameness.

If you ride such a horse too fast in an effort to supple and loosen him, then the problem will

Mouthing relaxes the muscles in the horse's entire body so that he can take up a contact.

only get greater. For riders moving from warmbloods to Barock type horses this weakness will be totally new and some find it difficult to deal with. Warmbloods often have a firm and straight back which has to be worked differently to ones with weak loins, arising out of a higher set on neck. In the case of warmbloods you usually only find this problem with long horses also with higher set on necks, such as Trakehners.

Riding the horse forwards and down with a lightly arched neck is a good way of strengthening the muscles.

Second variation

Another way of proceeding would consist of first of all riding the horse forwards and down, so that the poll is on a level with the withers and the neck is slightly arched. The nuchal ligament is shortened when the horse's nose is on or slightly behind the vertical – but always ensure that the legs are driving the horse forwards. This relieves the muscles of the hind quarters by at least 40 per cent since the withers are supported by the nuchal ligament. This is why the horse can be worked for longer periods of time in walk and trot without showing signs of tiredness. Longer periods of movement with smaller loads encourage muscle build-up and strength. If this all takes place at a quiet pace then the horse will remain relaxed.

At the start, it is possible that the horse may not move evenly. You have to accept this in the short-term. As soon as the horse is relatively steady in his contact, the rider should try to up the tempo – but only so far so that the horse can keep up a light contact. As training advances, the rider will find his horse's ideal working pace and from that form a good basis for further training.

Fundamentally, the horse should set his own working pace. If you watch a horse working from a very slow to a very fast tempo within a gait and observe him carefully you will be able to see that at a certain speed he will show a very round and even movement, while at either a faster or slower pace the contact will be inconsistent and he will likely show an irregular rhythm. The various tempos required later as a part of competition tests are a goal to aim at towards the end of training and not a tool during training.

If things start to fall to pieces when the horse is working, becoming more unsettled and faster when you ask him to move forwards, then the hindquarters are likely to be running after the horse's centre of gravity, i.e. his balance, in the true sense of the words. In this case you don't have the choice of making the hindquarters run faster since the rest of the horse is clearly already going too fast for the hindquarters to keep up. When you ask the horse to go slower than the hindquarters you create the effect of the horse coming back together and compacting up from behind. As a united whole it is then much easier to ask the hindquarters to take longer steps to increase the tempo, without the horse falling apart. If the quarters are put under too much strain as a result of going too fast, the horse will tend towards taking faster, but not longer, steps.

All these tips and hints are of course not a new discovery of classical riding, but rather tricks to help to bring a horse more easily back to classical dressage.

The raised hand when used carefully is a useful means to ask the horse to bend and work in a deeper outline.

The raised hand

I have already written about the effect of a raised hand in chapter 1, and especially here, when working on the basics of ridden work, it is of high value and an important aid on the way to developing an elegant and refined way of riding. It should however be used as an aid for education: first of all the rider must pay attention that he doesn't drop his hand before the horse has yielded – and also not immediately when the horse drops his nose and searches for the contact. If he did, then the horse would lift his nose up straight away when he felt the pressure of the bit on his tongue and the rider would correct him again, the horse would drop his nose, the rider would give with his hand… This can quickly develop into a yo-yo syndrome that never results in a steady contact.

Another way to use a lifted hand is for bending and flexing, since it helps the horse to find the way down with his head. To do this, flex the horse to the inside, using a higher inside hand, so that the poll and a third of his neck are in front of the raised rein and two thirds are behind it. You are literally bending the horse around the rein. The outside rein stays in a light but flexible contact with the mouth so that it can take over at any time. Since the horse will find it easier to stretch his back due to this bend, only stretching one side of his extensor muscles, then he will drop his head more easily.

Once the horse has dropped his head, the outside rein takes up the contact and the inside is released slightly, remaining responsible for the horse's straightness.

Rising trot with two variations

Rising trot has become an interesting tool. Most riders use it to be able to work the horse comfortably in trot, with the goal of warming the horse up or to relieve the horse's back.

There are though two types of rising trot referred to within German equestrian circles. The Prussian variation, which is today commonly referred to by all, regardless of country, as the rising trot, and the English trot, which has been lost in the mists of time.

We need to examine both variations and will begin with the original form, the English rising trot. The military description at the time was 'a light trot in an English style'. At the time everyone was aware of the left and right trot. In left trot, you stood up, when the left foreleg and the diagonally right hind moved forwards, in right trot then similarly when the right diagonal pair of legs (front right and left hind) moved forwards. When hacking out, you would swap between the two in order to ensure that one side didn't work more than the other. In a ménage, on the right rein you rode in right trot and on the left rein in left trot, meaning that you sat as the inside hind came forward. This resulted in the croup muscles on the inside being tightened faster and thus developed a greater ability to create forward impulsion. By doing this it would be possible to even out an irregular trot that is caused by a weaker hindleg.

By comparison, if going rising trot Prussian style, you would be sitting as the outside hind swings through – just as you would be going rising trot today. The Prussians carried out their cavalry drills at a very fast trot tempo and many of their horses cantered in the turns, which naturally interfered with the desired picture of total unity. For this reason, rising trot was introduced: in right trot the riders had to go rising trot as if they were on the left rein (i.e. the opposite of what they would normally do) and in left trot, go rising right. This meant that the horses were put out of balance and couldn't collect themselves, resulting in not being able to use the bend in the corner and the rider sitting down on their back to move into canter. It is for this reason that you need to be sitting when cantering out of a corner.

It makes a considerable difference, in terms of the effect of the rider on the horse, whether you are trotting in Prussian or English style. I first became

When rising in English trot the rider is standing up, as the inside fore is moving forwards.

When doing what we today call rising trot, the rider is out of the saddle as the outside fore swings forward.

aware of this difference when I was teaching beginners on the lunge at the start of my teaching career. They always started by rising on the 'wrong' leg and would have to correct themselves. On one rein in particular though I could see that the horse always came through better with his hindleg before the rider corrected herself, and then when the rider changed to the correct rise, the horse would always slightly drag the one hindleg and become less active in coming through. If I then got the rider to go rising 'incorrectly', the horse would always go better and more consistently. The rein on which this always seemed to happen most clearly was also the rein on which the horse found harder to canter on, which supported my theory that the English trot strengthens the inside hind.

You can put both variations of rising trot to good use: the Prussian version used today ensures that the horse can't move into canter as easily out of trot – you have to go sitting for a stride before asking for canter. This type of rising trot therefore helps to loosen up the horse in working trot and encourages him forwards.

If you want to ask the horse for a more collected trot or perhaps passage or piaffe in rising trot, then English style rising trot is the better choice. Here the rider is sitting on the inside hind, asking it to take up more weight and push his body more energetically forwards.

In half-pass, for example, it is possible to differentiate where a problem lies and then choose the appropriate form of rising trot. Where collection is lacking, the English rising trot is ridden, whilst where there is insufficient sideways movement then Prussian is the better option. In both cases the half-pass is improved with more expression and a better moment of suspension between strides.

On a circle you can most clearly see the supporting and strengthening effect that the English trot has. On a circle the horse will tend to fall into the centre when his weaker hindleg is to the inside and the rider has to constantly balance and correct. In addition, the horse will step through into the outside rein less than on the opposite rein. If you were to change from Prussian rising to English rising trot you would immediately notice that the problem lessens or even disappears and the horse will often appear to move with more energy.

Even if it does sometimes bother other riders to see a rider apparently rising on the 'wrong' leg, you should keep it up. It is better to have a horse that is moving evenly and rhythmically and is heading towards true straightness, than happy riding companions, who mostly know better than you anyway …

Returning to the example of the half-pass, here it is the inside hind that is the one responsible for the impulsion and the quality of the movement. By sitting on the outside hindleg, the inside hindleg can swing more easily forwards. Since though the rider's concentration of effort is placed on the outside hind, there is not going to be a good level of impulsion off the inside hind. The rider, in English trot, will be sitting though when the inside hindleg steps under, i.e. before it pushes off. By sitting on the inside hind the tension of the muscles there are increased and supports the actual mechanics of the movement.

The rider's axis of strength and balance and the horse's load-bearing axis have to be the same – otherwise it will be impossible for horse and rider to move together in harmony.

Also playing a significant role in the rising trot is the function of pushing or driving the horse forwards. Most riders use an active leg (i.e. to push or drive the horse on) as they sit and then open the leg as they rise. This is tolerated by most riding instructors, although I don't understand this at all. If you drive with your legs as you sit, then the leg is clamped in from the side and the seat from above. The rider is virtually pulling herself down into the saddle and is potentially blocking the movement. As she rises then she is standing in the stirrups and sticking the legs away from the horse so that it is feeling no aids. The rider's leg will likely appear unsteady and rough.

On the other hand if you were to drive as you rise, the leg will stay on the horse, encouraging the horse forwards and relieving the back, meaning it can swing freely. You can drive more than once in the stride which will encourage the hindleg through more. When sitting, the leg is relaxed and the movement won't be stopped by a leg that is clamped on. Above all, with lazy horses, using the leg as you rise is very important in encouraging the horse in the right way.

When used correctly, the whip should be used to touch not to punish.

The whip as a baton

The correct use of a whip should comprise of a light touch, not a punishment. Many riders use the whip too softly or too carefully whilst others go the other way and let rip – in each case it is usually used when the horse is being asking for more effort or forwards movement. When the whip causes pain however, the horse is more likely to tense up than be happy to move forwards. For the correct use you should observe the following rules:

• If you have to use a whip, then more has to result than would have if the aid was used without the support of the whip. Otherwise you run the risk of the horse always waiting for the whip aid before he does anything. And if you are not asking for more with the whip than without it, then for many horses you will need to use the whip more to achieve the same thing. Before reaching for the whip, it is always better to use one or two body, voice, seat or leg aids more strongly and then use the whip to emphasise and reinforce these.

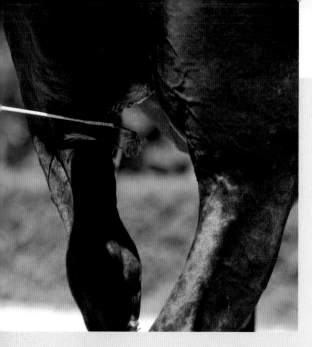

The whip can also be used in a targeted way from the ground to support the rider.

• The whip should not be used at the same time as the leg. Many riders clamp their legs on to their horse to push them forwards, at the same using the whip which runs up against the wall of the legs, as indeed does the movement. Gripping with the knees – something which is often encouraged – is anything but sensible. For this reason it is important that the leg is opened and then the whip applied. Only then can the horse move through into his shoulders and into the rider's hand.

• You should ideally get on the horse's nerves with the whip in order to really achieve your goal. By this I mean I would rather you tickled the horse with the whip several times than hit him hard once. Usually the whip transmits through to the mouth, because when the rider creates sudden impulsion he may sock the horse in the teeth, which doesn't exactly encourage the horse to go forward.

• The whip should always be carried on the inside – only then is it possible to use it to push him into the outside rein.

The canter – how and when?

The 'how' and the 'when' is the secret to a successful canter transition. To the question of, when is the right moment, I have one answer: when in trot you can almost feel or see the canter, then that is the time to ask for it.

The canter comes out of a half-halt (on the outside rein) so that the horse doesn't run into the canter but instead jumps forward and up, and above all takes more weight through the hindleg. To understand this better, we have to consider the biomechanics of the horse again. The half-halt in trot has the effect of blocking the outside shoulder and encouraging the inside hind to step through more underneath. Force results in a counter force, so the inside fore supports the hind by stepping forward more, because it has to replace the blocked outside foreleg and also catch the impulsion created by its diagonal hindleg.

The half-halt is sufficient as an aid to canter, although we all are aware of the many other aids that we were taught when learning to ride:

• Should you move your outside leg back? This results in the outside hind moving more forwards, which in turn means that the horse finds his take off leg more easily, allowing for the diagonal pair of legs to follow through in canter.

• Should you sit to the inside when asking for canter? This is supposed to help the horse to strike off on the correct leg. However, doing this means that you are not sitting on the horse's load-bearing axis (since when cantering this is located on the outside hand to enable the horse to jump

Here the horse responds well to the half-halt and strikes off correctly.

forwards). Secondly, by sitting to the inside you can also restrict the inside hind from moving through. For this reason it is more sensible to sit to the outside when asking for canter and only when the horse is in canter and the centre of gravity has moved to the inside, should you sit to the inside. I correct most horses that strike off on the wrong leg by asking the rider to sit more to the outside. As a result the horse is more likely to go sideways to the inside (on the correct leg) and not sideways to the outside (counter canter).

• Should you use the inside leg on the girth? This is supposed to encourage the inside shoulder to move up and through. This will only work though when the leg is held softly on the ribs and not clamped on or remaining glued to the side.

All these aids are correct, but only when used at the right time and in the right order – in other words, when they are necessary. Mostly, a correctly used half-halt is sufficient to get a transition to canter, possibly together with the inside leg used lightly, not heavily, to encourage the shoulder to explode forwards and to create tension in the muscles to the inside of the flanks.

There has already been much discussion about the correct seat when moving into canter – there are arguments for sitting to the inside just as there are for sitting to the outside. I see it as being quite simple: whatever works best and is most suited to my pupil's style of riding is fine, but if a horse can't canter properly then I help it by sitting to the outside.

Whenever I need a horse to jump through more under his centre of gravity then I would always sit initially to the outside. Once the horse can go in a collected canter, I sit to the inside when, for example, I want to work on making the pirouette smaller, or when I am working on canter half-pass, to encourage him more forwards and come through more from behind.

A half-halt can only work with a submissive and supple horse.

What is a half-halt?

Opinions differ here greatly when the question 'what exactly is a half-halt and, more importantly, what do I do when I want to ride one?' is asked. The theory says that you should ride the horse forwards into the hand – but what does that mean?

One of the prerequisites for a successful half-halt is that the horse is submissive and relaxed. Of course you have to be able to half-halt a horse that isn't relaxed but you would do this, for example, in trot by rising more slowly, and in walk and canter by closing the lower leg and breathing slowly through your nose.

You should work on the half-halt in walk first of all, to help the horse to begin to comprehend the aid. Using the lower leg you should ride the horse more into the hand, or in other words, into the contact, so that you feel more pressure from the contact in your hand. If the horse reacts by getting slower, open your hand slightly without losing the contact with his mouth – by doing this the horse will find it easier to carry himself. Continue to drive with your lower leg to prevent the horse from coming to a complete halt. If the horse accepts the aids, then repeat the exercise in trot.

To put the rider's body in the correct position he should move his knee slightly back when putting the aid on. This will be felt in the stomach and loin muscles, and at the same time will make the rider sit up more onto the seat bones which allows the horse to round his back more easily and carry the rider's weight better. If the rider tries to sit deeper in the saddle, the horse will also go slower because his movement is being interfered with. Usually then the horse will fall onto his forehand and lean on the bit. Consciously breathing slowly through the nose lifts the rider's breastbone in the right way – namely without hollowing the back.

The half-halt is the most important of all the aids, since by taking up more contact the horse sits more on his quarters and creates more expression in his movement, whilst still thinking forwards. But if you ride too many half-halts too strongly then the horse is likely to halt completely and stay standing.

The words 'half-halt' describe the exercise perfectly. The idea of coming half way to halting also expresses the sense that my horse is still moving forwards.

In German the word used is 'Parade' and they speak of a full Parade (i.e. a full halt) as well as a half Parade (half-halt). The full halt is ridden exactly the same as a half-halt with the difference that the aids are given faster, rather than being given more strongly with the hand and leg. Otherwise the horse would be hindered in its ability to balance itself and come through from behind. The hindquarters must be able to step through – if the rider's legs or more especially knees are clamped onto the horse, it will limit the ability of the shoulders to move as well as the ability of the forelegs to step forwards.

When giving a half-halt the rider must never get the feeling of falling down a hole. If a horse is carrying himself properly, this will mean that as a result of the movement in trot and canter the horse's body will almost float. The feet land on the ground before the weight of the horse starts to be felt and the horse's body follows it down. If the horse's feet land when the body has already started to 'fall', then the feet landing can be clearly heard, and it may be described as falling onto the forehand.

Improving the half-halt using the rocking chair

In advanced dressage the rocking chair exercise was removed to apparently avoid less than pretty sights since it would appear that many high level and apparently well trained dressage horses were not able to carry out this exercise. At this stage we should be asking what was wrong with them. This rocking exercise is the perfect way to move from walk to rein back – and any well trained horse should be able to manage to go from trot into rein back as well. In western riding a sliding stop would be impossible to carry out without using the same method as this exercise.

The basics of this are described in the next chapter.

The leg, moved back slightly, is the tool and main aid for the rocking exercise, in order to play with the horse's forwards and backwards movement. If the exercise is worked on correctly and not forced, the horse will learn to balance himself better, to collect himself and create more forwards energy. For this reason the rocking exercise is an indispensable means of preparing a horse that doesn't canter well or even one that can't do it all, for the canter. Expression and rhythm in the movement are both encouraged and the horse begins to dance, carrying both itself and its rider more easily. When, on the other hand, expression and rhythm are based on pressure and stress, then the horse is too tense to be able to rock.

Developing
basic tools
for ridden
work

There are exercises such as voltes, circles and so on and there are movements such as shoulder-in, half-pass and renvers. But then there are those that lie in between: tools that can help to opti- mise movement because they can help make an exercise or movement work more effectively.

The rein-back is ridden 'forwards' off the leg.

Rein-back as an example

To ask for a few steps of rein-back I will say to the rider that he should push his horse up into his hand from his calf until he is standing still, and then take care that he doesn't move forwards when he continues to push. You can clearly see question marks floating around the rider's head because he doesn't know what is going to happen…

And what does happen? The horse tries to walk forwards a couple of times but notices that he is confined so instead sits back on his haunches and steps back with good bend through his haunches and with a good and clear rhythm. The rider is pleasantly surprised, as his horse has probably never gone back so well before. Now to solve the puzzle: of course I have asked for the rein-back as an exercise but have not called it that, instead describing exactly what should be done. If I had simply said, 'now rein-back for several strides' the rider may well have tried to do this literally – usually by pulling on the reins. The horse will then often lift his head up above the reins, likely come to a grinding halt with his croup in the air. The horse is trying to avoid the pressure being put on him – and here again the magic word 'pressure' appears. The horse's first reaction will be counter-pressure as he doesn't want to give in. As a result, there is no degree of harmony.

Interestingly the above only works the first time, when the rider doesn't know what the end result is supposed to be. The second time he knows that he is supposed to rein-back. And when the horse doesn't go back as a result of the aid off the leg, the rider is likely to once again pull on the reins and the result is once again poor.

What I am trying to say is this: that the rider often puts a high value on being able to ride certain exercises and movements – the more and harder the better since it supposedly proves the

The horse is dropping his quarters and 'sitting' but because the rider is pulling back on the reins, the horse is resisting the hand.

rider's own ability. For the best result in the end though what is most and solely relevant is how the horse executes the movement and how his body works when doing it – reminding us of the old saying, which still applies today though we are always trying to re-invent the wheel: it's not arriving, but how you get there that's important.

To advance a horse in his training means being able to lead him along the right path. What is decisive in being able to do this is not using the usual and, perhaps, wrong techniques as a basis for his work, but instead looking for new and improved techniques to use. Only then will anything really change.

A rider shouldn't believe the myth that he can always control everything – for this he is lacking at least six arms and legs. In basic work the correct method and technique should be worked on so that this can later be built upon further. This will avoid having to resort to less desirable methods when you are riding at a higher level.

Strength and condition

Warming and loosening up is important, but a horse needs strength and condition in order to be able to learn technique.

I have a simple theory: if you cantered for the same amount of time that nowadays is spent in trot, but in a canter that is no faster than the trot, and if before you cantered you trotted for the same amount of time that is cantered, albeit at a slower pace, then most saddle fitters, vets and various other equine therapists would be out of a job.

With the help of clear flexion to the inside, the horse will drop his head more readily.

There can be no looseness if the horse doesn't have enough strength to carry out the work asked of him. But it is only when a muscle is loose that it can strengthen and be built up. The upshot of this rule is that you need to always fit the work to the amount of energy reserves that have been built up. If you constantly ask too much of a horse, then the individual muscle fibres will tear. It is true that up to five new fibres grow back, but together they won't have the strength of the single fibre that was there before. In addition, the damaged muscles have to be given time to rebuild before they can again be asked to stretch and build back up.

A horse trained to an average level of ability should be able to canter for up to half an hour with his rider; for a horse trained to a higher level this time will be proportionally longer. At this point we refer back to the knowledge gained from our investigation of biomechanics. We have learnt that the right positioning of head and neck will make it easier for the horse to step through under himself, at the same time also making the development of his strength equally easier. Therefore our first tool is the raised inside hand. Firstly, this helps to make the poll and neck more flexible and loose, and secondly,it causes the horse to more easily drop his head and neck since the raised hand can ask him to bend these around the inside rein as it is easier for him to stretch one side of his long back muscles than both at the same time.

It is important to be consistent when flexing the horse, even when initially the results are discouraging. This flexion should always come through from an upwards and forward action and never backwards towards the rider's chest. Once the horse has learnt the application of the raised inside hand, (see page 26) then he will yield.

If the horse really lets go through his poll and allows his neck to drop, then the rider needs to give instantly with the rein, take up the contact softly with the outside rein and straighten up the horse gradually. Small, gentle 'feels' on the inside rein will help the horse to relax and loosen. But watch out: too frequent and too firm tugs on the rein don't result in a better result – if the aid gets unpleasant for the horse then the opposite tends to happen.

A mistake that is often made is that the rider steadies himself by gripping too hard with his legs. Since this can cause a slight but uncomfortable pressure on the horse's shoulders, the horse will stiffen up and the exercise will fail. By comparison, a fine and repeated pressure from the calves, never the knees, will help to stimulate the abdominal muscles and will help the horse to find the right way of doing it.

Normally you would introduce anything new at walk and then later in trot, although there are horses that find it clearly easier to frame up and carry themselves in trot than in walk. In this case it is often better to try these exercises using the higher inside hand in trot. Later you can use this to improve flexion in its many forms, and particularly without losing the quality of movement. It can in fact improve the movement because the horse more readily relaxes.

Should a young horses have their nose in front of the vertical?

It is generally felt that young horses need to be ridden forwards so they take the rein down with their noses in front of the vertical. The other theory is that it makes more sense to ask for the nose to be behind the vertical.

In today's riding circles, unbreakable rules often grow out of superficial knowledge. Let's look at how this question might be worked through by using biomechanics as our knowledge base: asking a horse to stretch forwards and down appears to be logical when you know that in doing this his back will be stretched. But when his heavy head and neck is stretched too far forwards then this will move his centre of gravity forwards as well. This would cause the horse to work on his forehand if his quarters did not in turn step through underneath the horse. But a young, unbalanced and very likely weak horse, can't do this – possibly he could just about manage it on the lunge, but certainly not when ridden.

If you were to ask for the horse's nose to come behind rather than in front of the vertical, then the nuchal ligament would open and lift the withers forward, reducing the resistance that the quarters might meet in trying to reach through and under the horse, thereby allowing the horse to step through more.

Once the horse has got stronger and has learnt how to use his hindquarters better, then be can be asked to ride more in front of the vertical without losing either balance or the quality of the movement.

This young Friesian is heading in the right direction but is a bit too deep.

Now he has found the right position. A horse with such a short back must not be ridden too deep because he won't be able to relax.

The rule that says a horse should be ridden forwards to take the contact down has the purpose of checking how strong the horse is and his ability to take work, as well as checking what point we are in our training. So just as you can influence his head and neck, and through these his trunk, so you should also be able to shape and affect the development of his hindquarters. As a foundation for these we use the rein-back. (see page 86)

Just as you can influence his head and neck, and through these his trunk, so you should also be able to shape and effect the development of his quarters.

More collection leads to greater extension

The goal of the collecting exercises, and especially the work in piaffe and passage, is to encourage the horse to step underneath himself more with the help of the leg placed slightly further back. You could now object and say that you don't need any of these highly complicated exercises to do this. In any book on riding, you read that walk-trot transitions can help to collect a horse, and therefore also encourage the horse to step through underneath himself more with his hindlegs. The problem with this is that often these exercises can irritate the horse and make him tense. Often his relaxedness is lost when using this method and at the result may be that while you have a collected horse, you also have one that is set and tense.

I have given much thought to this problem. I have tried out the methods used by the old riding masters, who tend to start a horse in piaffe early on in an attempt get it to carry itself. Here though you quickly encounter the problem that the horse gets nervous and will repeatedly try to do piaffe-like steps in

his working trot, which is of course undesirable in a horse destined for competition.

Finally, I reached the conclusion that, as is often the case, the simplest and easiest way is best. When reining the horse back, you press your calves alternately on the horse, and when the horse begins to move back you move your legs slowly further back. I stop the horse moving back too fast by driving forwards lightly but energetically, albeit not so much so as to cause the horse to actually go forwards. The contact through the rein must be maintained. This starts interplay between forwards and backwards thinking in a horse. Or, to put it a different way, we might be riding rein-back transitions. The whip can also help to show the horse what we want by touching his leg to ask him to step forwards. When doing this your leg should be placed further back, the move with which the horse should learn to

Learning piaffe and passage help the horse to ...

... develop an extension that is forwards going with active hindquarters, but without getting faster.

Thanks to the aids from the leg, the horse is already lowering his quarters before the transition to walk.

At the beginning of his training this horse had shown no talent in his extension.

associate stepping more underneath himself and taking more weight through the quarters.

Let me illustrate this with an example. Many Barock horses, and also some warmbloods, lack an elevated trot – meaning they have only a short moment of suspension in their trot. The result of this is that often medium or extended trot is only, if at all, performed at much too fast a tempo.

If, though, I can encourage a horse to step more under himself by using a lower leg that is further back so that he floats like a swan on a lake, and does this from trot into walk – so I also ride my downwards transitions forwards – then I would also be able to get him back into my hand from an extended trot with my legs by quickly moving them back. I would then

get one or two big strides through the forehand with lots of expression. It is now important to immediately, and without a break, use the tension created to ask for more strides, at the same time carefully taking up more contact in the reins – in other words, rev him up a bit and do it again.

By doing this you will be able to create more extended steps. Then go back to working trot, so that the horse doesn't become overexcited. You need to repeat this exercise again and again over a number of weeks – not minutes! – until the horse understands the sequence of movements and can master it. The result and the tool you have created will play a significant role in the horse's training in the future.

Using **lateral movements** to develop collection

The ability of the horse to cross their legs, or rather move their body sideways, helps the horse towards self-carriage because these movements help to loosen up the horse's loins. At the same time, the hindleg, since it is stepping past the foreleg and forwards without any obstruction, will become freer in its movement, meaning that when going straight again the horse is better and more easily able to step under his centre of gravity.

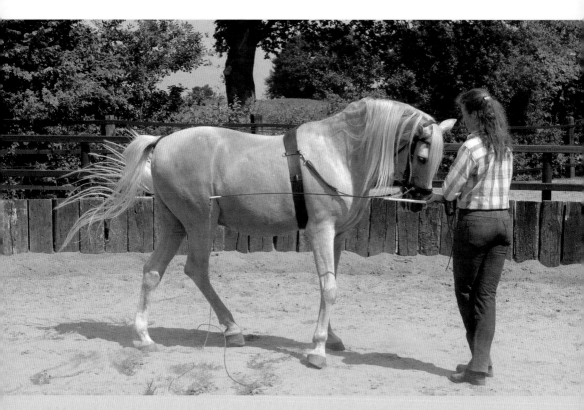

The exercise that is the foundation for all lateral movements: moving across in-hand. (Photo: Strocher)

The simplest version of this is to start to ask the horse to cross his legs over coming out of the turn on the forehand. It is important in terms of the quality and the affect of the exercise to find a way to start that is smooth and harmonious from the very beginning. When you don't have to use force, there can be no counter-force.

The turn on the forehand is perfect as the starting exercise for moving sideways and for the shoulder-in. Even travers and renvers can be worked on from this. We start in the middle of the circle as straight as possible and allow the horse to move slowly around the forehand with the hind quarters.

Asking for lateral movement in-hand

Working on lateral steps in-hand is the foundation for much of the in-hand work to be done later. With the horse standing on the lunge in front of me, I touch it on the flanks with my whip so that it moves several steps to the side. I then send him back onto the track and continue to work it on the lunge.

At a later opportunity I will repeat on the other rein so that the horse takes a few steps to the right or left each time. This exercise is also well suited for unruly stallions since it reinforces the higher ranking position of the person lungeing. Ensure that the horse gives with his quarters first and stays relatively straight through his body, so that he doesn't drift out through his outside shoulder. You should start this initial work on a circle and then move to the outside track, not asking for the sideways movement step by step, but instead repeatedly building up enough impulsion so that he takes a few lateral steps by himself. This should be repeated to make the movement more fluid.

As soon as the horse has learnt to take a few lateral steps on the lunge, you can start to really work on this in-hand. You should use a shorter (3 metre) lunge line which attaches to a cavesson. The horse should also be fitted with side reins, a bridle and a surcingle, and have been warmed up thoroughly on the lunge before starting. Start by asking him to step across on the left rein. Work out of a circle onto the long side, working on the inside track and continuing to lead the horse on the left rein.

The lunge line should be held with the left hand, the lunge whip with the right, but held horizontally on the horse's left side, and you should touch the whip to the horse's quarters positioned on the outside track. The forehand continues on the inside track, but the horse should be straight through the head neck and body. On the next circuit ask for the horse to flex to the inside so that you start to develop shoulder-in. Pay attention that the hindquarters remain on the outside track and that the hindlegs do not cross over, as then the horse will be bending through his ribs which is not what we want at this stage.

The horse must of course cross his forelegs over and ideally he should be doing this between the two tracks. Seen from behind, three legs should be visible, these being both hindlegs and the inside fore. The outside fore is hidden by the inside hindleg so that the horse is therefore moving on three tracks.

When this can be done successfully on both reins, try counter shoulder-in. To do this, the horse is worked exactly the same as with shoulder-in but with the handler and the horse bent to the outside. Counter shoulder-in is easier to do than shoulder-in because the horse is confined to the outside by the arena or ménage fence and no longer – as is the case with shoulder-in – by the handler alone. In spite of this you should always work on the shoulder-in before the counter shoulder-in in order to reinforce the required obedience on the lunge.

In contrast to the shoulder-in, which can be done on circles and even through the corners, in the opposing exercise you should not go deep into the corners, and even round them off a bit or go straight, albeit flexed to the outside through the corners at the start to make it easier for the younger horse. In this exercise the younger horse will be working into the outside rein for the first time and will begin to collect itself. This will be a new experience for the youngster. For this reason take plenty of time to work through this quietly. The exercises described above are the foundation for all further lateral work.

To prepare for working towards half-pass the horse should also be asked for lateral steps when changing rein across the diagonal, if possible with the nose turned slightly towards the direction of movement.

More on this subject can be found in my book 'Handbook of long-reining'.

When moving across laterally the horse should be straight, with only a hint of flexion and bend to the inside.

Riding lateral movements

The first steps of lateral work under saddle – just as when working in-hand - should be in the form of a turn of the forehand. It is very important that the horse is working into the outside rein. You should give small half-halts on the inside rein and use your inside leg and the whip to encourage the horse to move across. All attempts by the horse to escape forwards should be stopped by the outside rein. The half-halts are important as these will prevent the horse from setting his head and neck. If the horse does block, which isn't unusual, allow him to take a few steps forwards before starting again. You should only be satisfied once the horse

has taken several good independent steps, with clear crossing over of the legs.

After a few days, start to work on these steps, moving out of the turn on the forehand by giving with the outside rein and asking more through the leg to encourage the horse's hindleg to cross further, so that the horse also moves his forelegs across. When doing this you will need to watch that the horse doesn't get faster in the forelegs than the hindlegs, as then the rider risks losing control of the shoulders. The rider can only really ly hold on to the inside rein in such a case, which doesn't help the development of the exercise.

Once you have managed to ride the turn on the forehands forwards, and widened the movement out into an arc on a circle, ask the horse for a greater angle so that in the end the horse is working at a 70° angle to the line of the circle. By doing this, the forehand and hindquarters are stretched and loosened, both of which are important if you are later hoping for a spectacular half-pass from your horse.

At only a slight angle, the hindleg will step well under the horse's centre of gravity without being directly linked in terms of a line of force with the forehand. This especially helps larger horses to square up and carry themselves. At an angle of 70° and more, the horse will become more collected, leading to the development of a new improved cadence and balance in the movement.

If you make the mistake of bending the horse through his length (or longitudinal axis), then you lose the benefit of the movement because the horse will fold up like a pocket knife and fall out through his shoulder back towards the outside track.

In summary, asking horses to move across laterally, or to leg-yield, will develop a new quality to his paces. Of course the training of the movements will help to shape the horse, but from a training point of view the value of the exercises is more to improve the mechanics of movement in the horse's body.

The value of the exercise can be increased dramatically by working a bit on it every day in walk, trot and canter to perfect it further, using different tempos and transitions within and between the paces, similar to the way a boxer might go running every morning before starting his workout.

Being consistent in the way this exercise is done – in other words asking enough but not too much from your horse – is the happy medium that leads to success. Remember though that to know where exactly the boundary is, sometimes you have to test it and even step over it. Harmony and elegance should always be visible, even when stepping over the line; for to quote my great hero Fredy Knie Sr. to whom I owe so much, 'Dressage is making love for the eyes'.

Shoulder-in

The old masters said that the shoulder-in 'helps and prevents everything'. In my opinion this may have come from their enthusiasm of discovering

The shoulder-in is a bending exercise and not truly a lateral movement. When riding on more than three tracks it loses this bending effect.

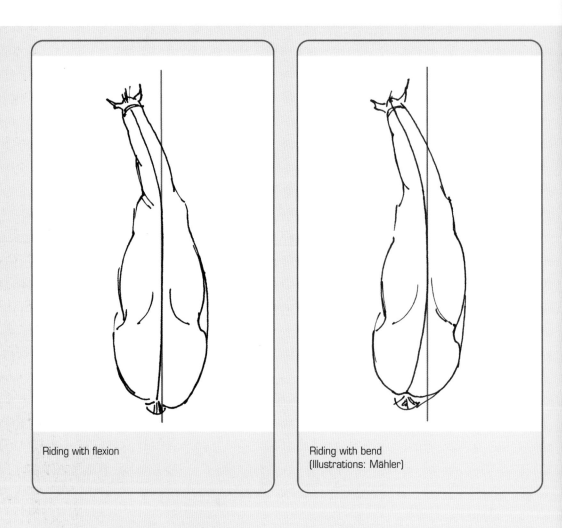

Riding with flexion

Riding with bend
(Illustrations: Mähler)

it, though in truth if it didn't already exist it would have to be invented. No other exercise or movement helps the horse quite so much to balance and to collect with real benefits for the expression in its movement.

Riding in flexion is a very helpful exercise as preparation. On the one hand, it helps the horse to bend around the inside leg even in its simplest form. On the other hand, it can be taken further by asking for the quarters to move onto the same line as the forehand and creating inside bend.

This second variation is a good preparation for travers.

Shoulder-in will only help though if ridden correctly. If the horse is allowed to have all four feet on the track with the rider trying to pull the shoulder-in with the inside rein, at the same time perhaps sitting to the inside, then the rider will be riding the classic head-in...

By riding like this the most you will achieve will be to put the horse totally out of balance. If at the same time you are riding too fast, as the horse

Canter shoulder-in: an exercise in balance.

offers speed since he is trying to run to catch up with his centre of gravity, then the effort to ride shoulder-in will end in catastrophe.

This catalogue of mistakes is no understatement, and meant in all seriousness. Often shoulder-in is seen as one of the lateral movements and ridden as such. But shoulder-in is a bending exercise, with more in common with the circle or volte. It is true that it is easier to ride out of lateral steps than out of a circle, since the transition from a volte to shoulder-in is difficult and demands a change in direction for a horse. By comparison, once I have asked the horse for a few steps of lateral movement I just have to go straight and allow less and less angle, while at the same time asking for more forwards.

'The horse must be straight on curved lines' is an oft-repeated phrase heard during a horse's training. By doing this, the horse's impulsion from his hindquarters can move through his entire body to the poll via the forehand. A second important requirement is to 'bend the horse on straight lines' because it helps the horse maintain its balance and to grasp new things more easily. In addition, it is less likely to fall out through its shoulder, meaning the rider will not have to correct the horse as much.

Later, when riding shoulder-in on the outside track, the rider will turn his upper body thinking 'inside shoulder back', without tipping back. He should be riding the horse with both legs into the outside hand. If it loses flexion through the poll, which is what is telling the horse's hindquarters which side his ribs should be bending to, then the rider should lift the inside hand to correct this flexion. After the correction, the inside rein should be on a lighter contact than the outside rein, which is asking the shoulder to move over – hence the name 'shoulder-in'. At the same time you should be driving evenly with both legs, not really to increase the pace but rather to steady.

Once you can swap between leg-yielding down the outside track and riding shoulder-in on three and four tracks – at least in walk and trot but ideally in canter too – then the time is ripe for starting the half-pass and pirouette.

Using lateral work as a foundation for working towards flying changes and pirouettes

Starting work on lateral movements marks a new phase in a horse's training, as we start to change the very nature of his movement. The horse develops more cadence and rhythm in his movement due to it stepping more underneath itself and creating more impulsion. Travers and half-pass are the best ways to utilise both the ability to collect and the cadence developed by the shoulder-in. But lateral work is also key for developing canter changes and pirouettes.

An important rule when working on lateral paces is that 'lateral work should never be ridden laterally'. Instead it should be ridden out of forwards movement.

When working on travers you should leave yourself plenty of time and be precise in your training of the finer points. In the Spanish Riding School in Vienna there are a sequence of exercises in which all of the basic lessons are included – I call it the 'gymnastic sequence'.

This sequence of exercises begins by riding shoulder-in on the inside track down the long side. Halfway down (i.e. at either E or B) straighten the horse but stay on the two tracks the horse has been moving on in shoulder-in. Then, using what was previously the inside rein and the outside leg, ask for outside bend, creating renvers out of what was shoulder-in, with the former inner rein producing half-halts to keep the quarters on the track. If you were to use the leg too strongly the horse would lose the bend and flexion because

The crossing over of the legs whilst holding a good bend causes many horses problems. To help the horse, let it lead slightly with his quarters rather than the shoulder.

Travers is a valuable exercise for improving cadence and should be worked on thoroughly.

it would shorten up the muscles in his quarters to the outside rather than the inside. What was previously the outside leg is responsible for the new bend and asks the hindleg to move through under the horse's centre of gravity.

The good thing about this transition between shoulder-in and renvers is not so much the change required in effort and bend, in other words true lateral movement, but more that the flying change from canter to counter canter is hidden within this exercise. The advantage is that, thanks to the shoulder-in, the horse's hindlegs are close together, balanced and in cadence. By changing the bend under the rider, not as so often before in front or

A loose inside rein – this is especially important when working laterally.

behind the rider, the change can take place more easily and securely.

But let's go back to our gymnastic sequence. At the corner after the long side the horse should be moved out of renvers into counter shoulder-in by maintaining the bend from renvers and changing the sideways steps, for example from left to right in renvers to stepping from right to left. This is achieved primarily by the turning of the rider's body. In renvers the rider has moved his body, thinking 'outside shoulder back'. The change to counter shoulder-in though is achieved by the rider turning his body this time thinking 'inside shoulder back'.

For renvers on the left rein this means that the rider moves his left shoulder back, while in changing over to counter shoulder-in he turns his body so that the right shoulder is moved back. Since the horse's bend doesn't actually change, the aids through the legs and reins for bend and forwards impulsion remain the same. The bend and forwards impulsion is created with the inside leg and as a correction the inside rein. The outside rein keeps the horse on the correct track and the inside rein is used very carefully to support the outside rein. Now we have reached a point that deserves special attention: it is the outside rein and not the leg that plays the main role, whilst on the inside it is the other way around with the leg doing most of the work and not the rein.

> In classical dressage it is always the case that an exercise must be developed and built up so that it can be ridden with the outside rein and the inside leg.

In the case of impatient riders you often see this the other way around; the inside rein and the outside leg dominate because supposedly this makes the horse go faster. In reality this just means that the horse is likely to be bent to the wrong side and the inside shoulder will be blocked by the inside rein, resulting in a loss of impulsion. What particularly works to the detriment of exercises in the future, such as pirouette and flying changes that help to develop lateral work, is the use of a sideways driving, heavy outside leg. This will have the effect of pushing him off balance so that he won't be stepping through forwards and sideways into the outside rein and under his centre of gravity, but instead will just step sideways, without the accompanying forwards movement. This will mean that later when doing flying changes, the horse will not change and jump forwards, but instead move to the side, usually with the quarters changing first. In the case of pirouettes the results are even more serious, as the sideways movement will mean that the horse will not be able to find the point of rotation needed for the movement. This will mean that the hindleg will lead the pirouette, rather than the forehand moving around the quarters.

In the half-pass you often see the quarters leading the forehand from the start. This too can be put down to incorrect aids. Neither cadence nor rhythm can really develop because the movement and the impulsion can't go through the horse's body into the outside rein.

The next step in the gymnastic sequence is the transition from counter shoulder-in to travers. In effect this involves the same sequence as going from shoulder-in to renvers. Starting on the short side, change the bend but not the leg crossing in the corner before the second long side so that counter shoulder-in changes to travers. The horse should be straightened with the old outside rein and collected with the old inside, or rather the new outside rein using half-halts. The new inside leg maintains the bend and the new outside leg holds but doesn't push the hindquarters in the new direction. If it did then the horse's body wouldn't be put into travers through this body, but rather the quarters would just be moved to the inside without the necessary forwards movement and with the bend through the ribs also likely being lost. This exercise has the flying change to the inside hidden within it , but only as already indicated, as long as the change in the bend is created by the rider's outside leg forwards rather than sideways.

Now continue to ride travers almost to the end of the long side, when the rider turns his body more to the outside, thinking 'outside shoulder back' in order to ride onto a small half circle – this exercise is called 'passat'. In order to be able to ride such a tight turn around the quarters, you will need to half-halt repeatedly on the outside rein. By doing this the hindquarters will step well under and the forehand will move to the inside

Trot half-pass into the canter pirouettehalf-passso that more forward momentum is created ...

... before it is turned energetically in a canter pirouette.

providing the horse is clearly bent around the inside leg.

The passat contains the beginnings of the pirouette. It can be ridden in trot and canter assuming the right degree of training. This exercise when ridden in trot will also introduce the beginnings of the technique for the piaffe, because as a result of the tight turn and the

requirement for the horse to really step under and around his hindquarters, he will begin to piaffe automatically – forwards and to the side – so that he doesn't have to hold the tension through the entire body.

When doing this exercise correctly for the first time many horses react with reluctance and resistance. I always used to think that this came from

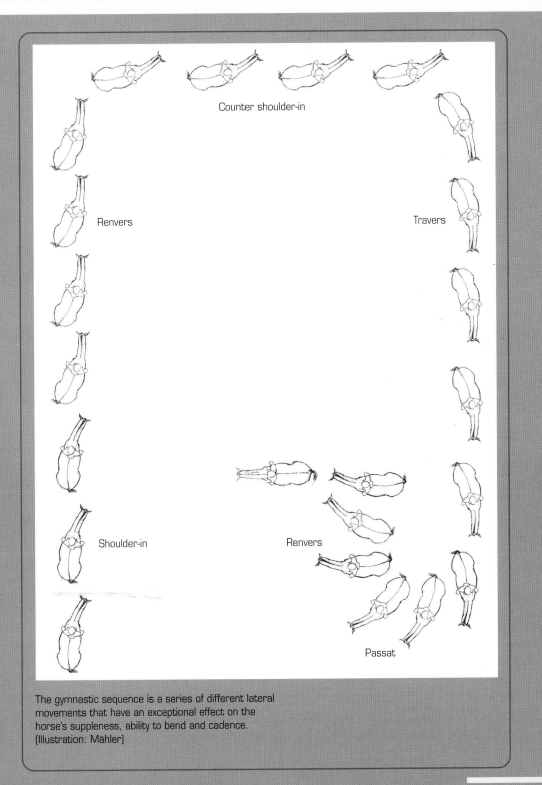

Counter shoulder-in

Renvers

Travers

Shoulder-in

Renvers

Passat

The gymnastic sequence is a series of different lateral movements that have an exceptional effect on the horse's suppleness, ability to bend and cadence. (Illustration: Mähler)

the additional effort that the horse is being asked for. Today, though, I think I have found the real reason which is that when the horse bends correctly around the inside leg, and at the same time the inside hindleg and the inside hip are being moved across towards the inside fore, then the horse is bent like never before under the saddle. The inside panel in the case of most English saddles will be pressed into the inside back muscles, and with wedge shaped panels the resulting pressure will be very high – the horse isn't used to this and is likely to show it. When you consider it, you can often see the same horse happily performing pirouettes in the field without any problem whatsoever while refusing to do it when ridden.

At the end of the gymnastic sequence the renvers is ridden on a line parallel to the long side. Using the outside rein the last few stride are increased so that the horse stands parallel to the short side, but looking towards the new direction. Now you can practice the exercises on the other rein in the same order.

Now let us summarise all of this: this sequence of exercises offers everything from shoulder-in to the start of canter changes, and the passat in trot gives the horse a taste of piaffe. Above all though, horses that tense up easily are being well prepared for collected work. When you can ride the passat in canter this is the perfect preparation for the canter pirouette. Even when horses have problems maintaining their rhythm, or the hindleg sticks in the pirouette, this exercise is helpful for working on the technique needed for the pirouette without causing the horse stress.

The gymnastic sequence should be used daily – first in walk and later, when the horse can achieve this comfortably, in trot and finally canter. The trot work especially will help horses that have problems with the canter as usually they are lacking balance and the strength needed for collection.

Counter canter

The renvers plays a key role in the preparation for and execution of the counter canter, since in renvers the horse learns the correct bend and

Well prepared by the renvers, the horse is able to strike off in counter canter on the circle.

108

balance that it needs for the counter canter. The counter canter is a simple exercise for the horse, providing that it is begun at the right time. But for the rider it is quite difficult, because he has to have learnt to sit correctly and to ride straight on curved lines. Most horses don't care whether they lead with the inside or outside leg. If, however, the rider puts weight through the outside, he will get an inside canter. Why? When the rider sits to the outside, the horse is pushed to the inside and will usually lead correspondingly with the inside leg. At the same time the horse is often held too strongly through the inside rein, which

Perfect – a hint of renvers in the counter canter.

Here the horse is cantering 'into the wall' making the counter canter difficult to ride.

109

pushes him towards the outside track and into the fence or wall, opening the inside shoulder and again causing the inside lead.

The correct preparation for counter canter would be renvers, which unfortunately hardly any riding school pupil or riding school horse knows how to do. Riding in renvers will put the rider in the right place in the saddle, and the horse will also have the correct bend and flexion to be able to strike-off correctly. A half-halt on the outside rein when in the renvers should be sufficient to ask for the canter transition. The horse will have already got used to the half-halt in canter, so the rider should sit as if riding renvers when asking for counter canter in order to help the horse, and then sit straight so as not to upset the horse's balance.

Counter canter ridden on a circle has its own special problems due to the line of the circle that the horse has to follow. If the horse has difficulties with this then the rider can help by sitting to the inside and slightly forward in order to push the horse's outside shoulder into the circle, which should make it easier for the horse to stay on the circle.

In my opinion, you should work on the flying change before the counter canter. There are however exceptions to this: a horse that, despite being able to cope with the lateral exercises, doesn't have good balance, may find that the counter canter on a circle will give it more strength and the ability to straighten – which in turn will help when working towards the flying change. In addition, there are many horses that clearly find it easier to change from the outside to the inside, so a secure counter canter can be a good starting point for the flying change.

Half-pass

The movement when the horse is going forwards and sideways diagonally across the arena is called the half-pass, the preparation for which is the travers. In the half-pass though there is more forwards movement required than is asked for in the travers, with the impulsion and the weight bearing ability of the inside hindleg working together with good bend through the ribs to moving in the direction of the bend. The half-pass has nothing to do with the leg-yielding, in which the sideways movement dominates.

The half-pass is begun at the start of the long side by flexing the horse to the inside. The rider turns his upper body while thinking 'outside shoulder back' in his mind. By doing this the rider will sit in such a way that the horse moves his quarters in and by doing do so will move laterally. The turning of the upper body needs to be maintained, but the rider also needs to sit upright and slightly forwards in the direction of the movement in order to encourage the horse further. He shouldn't sit to the inside from the start though, as in doing this he would be sitting against the movement – this is because at the start the horse is moving straight ahead and not in half-pass. The inside leg needs to drive the horse forwards into the outside rein, through which half-halts can also be given to increase the degree of the half-pass.

With horses that have problems bending towards the direction of the movement and stepping sideways, it may be helpful to turn out of the corner into passat, and then try to develop the half-pass back to the long side. The horse will find it encouraging to see the long side coming

The half-pass requires impulsion and bend, and the hindquarters must be able to carry the horse easily.

up in front of him. In addition, the passat places the horse's quarters so that they are leading slightly, which also helps the horse to hold the bend. The most frequent problems encountered in the half-pass are:

• The bend through the neck and body is incorrect. Usually the cause is found in a lack of bend through the ribs.

To improve this it can help to ride a volte before starting the half-pass, in other words developing a better reaction to the inside leg by riding shoulder-in and voltes. Many instructors teach the half-pass out of the shoulder-in. Without a doubt, this can be a great help in terms of achieving the correct bend and flexion. However, caution is advised, as when riding

The rider sits up straight in the direction of the movement in order to encourage the horse forwards and sideways into the half-pass.

dressage tests in competition you can't use the shoulder-in for this purpose. In shoulder-in on the left rein, the horse is crossing from left to right, but in the half-pass from right to left. The transition that is necessary to move from one to the other in trot and canter can be seen as an irregularity in pace, and the horse's expression can also suffer at the moment of transition – since the new direction in which the legs are crossing over means the role of the hindlegs are swapped (one being used to push off and the other catching the impulsion). Finally, the half-pass should appear like a phoenix from the ashes, and with more impulsion become more expressive.

• The horse loses the bend and the sideways movement towards the end of the half-pass.

Usually the rider responds incorrectly by trying to flex the horse more, using the inside rein to recreate the bend. However, the horse will be running out of energy by this stage, and with it its balance. It is therefore trying to straighten out and get back to the outside track as fast as it can, or may also try to bend in the opposite direction, going out through its shoulder back to the track. Once this problem arises then this half-pass can't usually be saved – it is better to stop trying and just ride forwards in a straight line parallel to the long side and then start again. When starting again you should intentionally position the quarters so they are leading slightly in order to help the horse hold the bend. The hindleg is asked to step across in front of the line of force so that the sideways momentum isn't directed through the horse's entire body. This makes the sideways movement easier and the horse won't resist as much. Later you can return to a more correct position but in the meantime you are saving both a fight and tension occurring in the half-pass.

• The half-pass isn't concluded correctly.

One of the most important points that should be paid attention to from the start is the correct ending of the half-pass, which means ensuring that when the horse gets back to the track that the quarters are a touch in front of the shoulder. If a rider isn't careful and consistent at this stage it will make riding a flying change after the half-pass notably harder later on. Those horses that find flying changes easy will try to change early and then hug the track, while the horses that

The inside hand that asks for the flexion can help the horse greatly, although most attention should be paid to the inside leg.

don't change easily won't, since they are likely to have gone straight too early while still on the line of the half-pass. If you have a horse that has weak quarters and are trying to work on zig-zag half-passes with changes between direction, by not placing enough value on correctness early on you will have shut the door on a good and easy way of training the movement later.

• Nervous horses often begin to rush sideways when starting the half-pass.

Here you will need to correct the horse by driving much more forwards with the inside leg whilst half-halting on the inside rein.

Zig-zag half-passes

Many riders tend to allow their horse to lead with the quarters, which can detract from both the movement and the expression. Zig-zag half-passes can help when working on this problem. Zig-zag half-passes are ridden by doing half-pass right for a few steps, and then half-pass left for the same number of paces, the secret lying in the change of direction. The half-pass needs to be stepped up at the end so that all you have to do is to ride the horse around the new inside leg to be able to move into the next half-pass in the other direction. The rider has to almost ride a quarter of a 10 metre circle forwards in order to create the new half-pass out of the forwards momentum already created. As in many cases, with riding the transition the most important thing is for the movement to be carried out correctly. You should ride the horse around the appropriate inside leg in a half 10m circle in order to position the horse into the new half-pass.

The half-pass helps to improve the horse's expression in trot and is the first step towards passage for many horses – but only when the horse is ridden forwards rather than sideways. Zig-zag half-passes are an advancement and progression of the half-pass and so can also have an improving effect on cadence and collection.

Creating more cadence and expression through the forehand

Lateral movements give us the chance to have a specific influence on our horse. Training a horse also means producing certain feelings in our horses and then working with those feelings. The following exercises work using a similar script. The goal is to wake the horse up and motivate it to bring more expression into its movements, and to encourage his talent to dance. To begin with, we will be riding the sequence of exercises in walk as practice, but for them to be really effective they will need to be ridden in trot and canter.

Begin by riding shoulder-in down the long side. At the end of the long side go straight into passat and then ride in renvers back to the outside track. Once back at the other end of the long side ride a half circle in the corner and start to ask for some extension as much as is possible back to the track. Once you are back on the outside track the horse should be ridden into the shoulder-in with the outside rein using all the energy created through the extension. The horse will come back to you as a result of the shoulder-in and will therefore show a lot of cadence in the forehand in the first few steps.

It is exactly this alternation between the shoulder-in (which has a loosening and suppling effect) at the start of the exercise, then the heavily collecting effect of the passat, followed by the collection of the renvers (which causes the horse to want to think forwards). We allow this by asking for extension into and out of the corner in order then to use the impulsion back into the shoulder-in to create more cadence in the collection again.

More cadence in movement: the result of a good half-pass.

It improves the quality of the paces greatly, riding into the corner in collection and coming out of it in extension – the horse begins to literally float into the corner.

The exercise should be repeated five to ten times, firstly in trot and later in canter. But you should always remember to stop before the horse gets tired or bored. The exercise is only ridden at walk to help learn it.

Alternating between shoulder-in and half-pass is a good way to improve the activity of the hindlegs.

Developing 'throughness' in the ribs and loins

When a horse doesn't take up a good contact, it is often lacking impulsion or it is lacking the looseness in his body to allow forth impulsion created from behind into the hand. Frequently these types of horses are stiff through their ribs and loins.

In this case an effective exercise to use is started at walk until the horse has understood the sequence of movements involved. Start by riding a half-pass out of a corner across the diagonal, but after three or four strides change into shoulder-in on a line parallel to the long side. And again after three or four strides ride forwards using both legs into the half-pass again. This change from one to the other should be down across the length of the diagonal. It is most effective in trot and canter. For even more effect go rising trot in the half-pass and English rising trot in the shoulder-in.

The change from shoulder-in to half-pass with the same bend will especially loosen up the loins, but will also make the horse more supple through the ribs. The bend stays the same and the horse is still bent around the inside leg. It is important that you ride off the inside leg every time you change from one to the other, as with each change the way the horse crosses its legs changes, and this alteration to the rhythm also has a suppling effect.

**What to do when the horse leans
on the bit**

You often see horses leaning on the bit
when they are coming more through
from behind. Usually the rider will react
in the wrong way by tugging or even
pulling the horse's head up, resulting in
the horse immediately stiffening in its
back and shoulders. If instead he lifted
his hands to raise the bit without pulling
on the mouth and without a loss of contact, then the horse is likely to give
through the poll, which had stiffened by
leaning on the rider's hands, and may
even swing through the back more. The
horse lifts up off the bit because the
pressure from the bit is lifted from the
tongue up to the corner of the mouth,
briefly causing the horse to open its
mouth. The shoulder and back will also
be loosened, and in any case the horse
will show more expression through the
forehand using this type of correction.
In principle this correction is nothing
more than a half-halt which is like a bit of
a shake, without losing the contact. The
horse will continue to pull into the hand
which is however indispensable for a constant improvement.

If a horse is leaning on the bit when working on collection, then you will need to
'shake' the horse off the hand by intentionally breaking the contact with the
horse's mouth, but at the same time neither pulling nor tugging since that would
cause the back and loins to tense up, In
collection the horse is in effect standing
on a smaller area so needs his head and
neck to help him balance. This is why the
contact has to be repeatedly and briefly
given away. In the case of extended work
or work at faster speeds, the connection
through the reins tends to be somewhat
stronger so the horse can be encouraged to step through from behind into
the hand.

The **flying change** as a valuable tool

The flying change is basically just a change of rein or direction. However, it conceals many dangers, and the experts argue about whether the flying change should be taught early on or later in a horse's education.

Fundamentally all movements are training tools, which by appropriate use at every stage of training should help a horse to develop. Some of these movements should not, as is done by many trainers, be treated as something holy and award a rider a medal when he rides his first flying change correctly. This will only stop the rider advancing and makes training the horse more difficult. Flying changes in particular can help to loosen and supple a horse in a particular way.

When is the right time to introduce them?

Those advocating the later introduction of flying changes justify their view by saying that at the lower levels of dressage competition you wouldn't want the horse to change by mistake and ruin the test. I find this ridiculous. If this was the case, then that would mean in effect telling the horse that in preliminary and novice dressage tests counter canter and flying changes are bad mistakes to make, only so that the horse could not misunderstand sloppily given canter aids and ensure that it always canters on the correct leg. Later, when the horse progresses to elementary, the statement about counter canter no longer holds, but the canter change remains a 'non-movement'. And finally, even later in the training, the statement about the flying change is again withdrawn.

The way you handle a young dog can be compared with this rather questionable 'training logic'. As long as he is small and cute he can chew shoes. Once he is older and no longer as cute, suddenly he gets punished for chewing them. How is the animal supposed to recognise and understand this logic, when none exists?

I think that it is fundamentally better to start this movement before the counter canter is secured, but after working on lateral movements, since the lateral movements are as good a preparation for the canter as the changes are. The exception to this are horses that from an early stage have done flying changes of their own will because they have, for example, greater problems with their balance and this change of leg is need-ed to maintain fluidity in their work rather than always changing down through trot and back up to canter. There are also horses that are so secure in their flying changes that they use them against the rider by changing in order to intentionally upset the rhythm. Only with great skill can the flying change be used as a tool with this last type of horse.

Working towards the flying change

The first prerequisite for performing a flying change is that the horse is capable of working at different tempi and at varying levels of collection. The horse should be able to canter up into the hand– an aspect that is often forgotten since in the horse's basic training the horse is worked more off the hand. As a direct preparation for the canter change you should work the horse into the hand, in order to be able to confine the horse during the initial changes and be able to better control it. If you don't do this preparation, the horse will often take off when changing, becoming far too fast and literally jumping into the contact. In this case a loose rein is a hard rein because the horse is unable to predict it.

On suppling lines

Probably the best way to develop the flying change is by using lateral movements. As already mentioned in the previous chapter, you can work on the change from inside (i.e. correct lead) to counter canter by using the transition from shoulder-in renvers on the first third of the long side. Over the last third of the long side put the horse back into shoulder-in and change back to the inside lead.

Thanks to the sideways tendency of the canter the horse is easier to keep both collected and narrow behind. If you then change from shoulder-in to renvers the sideways tendency is maintained but the bend is changed, which is what causes the canter leg change. Afterwards, the horse is bent around the inside leg for shoulder-in and to achieve the change of leg back to the inside. In order to get this right the horse must be ridden into the outside hand from the inside leg and of course be appropriately prepared first in walk and trot.

The change from an inside to an outside canter lead is worked on by using the transition from shoulder-in to renvers.

Riding a half ten metre circle from the corner marker and returning to the track

Horses that are well balanced and have a good level of collection may find it easier to work on the flying change by using a half circle ridden out of the corner to then return to the track. It is important not to make the turn too large or return to the long side at too sharp an angle. On returning to the track the horse should be flexed into the new bend by your leg and rein, which should result in the change. The turn out of the corner helps to collect the horse through its quarters, and on reaching the track you should wait to change the bend and ask for it only once the entire horse is back on the track. With horses that can't wait for the aid to come from its rider you should ride back to the track on the long side almost as if in travers, intentionally allowing the quarters to lead and thus preventing the horse

Flying change out of half-pass

As already described, the half-pass is a good start-ing point for the flying change – especially when a horse is lacking a dynamic canter and often has problems with canter changes. Ride a half-pass starting at the top of a long side across to the cen-tre line, with the quarters and shoulders arriving at the same time. Now ride on in a straight line and push the quarters when coming out of left half-pass to the right. Together with a half-halt and a straight and lifted forehand, this should cause the horse to change. As a result of the half-pass the horse should be well collected and in self-car-riage, and when it reaches X the straightening and then the flexion to the new rein should be enough to cause the flying change. Pushing the hindquar-ters over into the new direction also offers the horse further help. You must watch though not to ride the half-pass sideways, and instead forwards as otherwise the horse will wobble back and forth in the changes. This is especially the case when you later try to ride half-passes back and forth in a zig-zag.

Using a working canter pirouette

This exercise is used when the counter canter has been too well established too early on so that the horse makes no effort at all to change. In the pirouette the horse is very collected, so that he is working on a very small area and will thus be more susceptible to the effects of the rider chang-ing his balance, which can then result in a flying change. When trying pirouettes for the first time, a horse will often change behind when you ask for too much turn. This can be used by changing direction directly out of the pirouette and giving

from changing the lead early. When trying to change the horse will try to bring the quarters in, in other words more renvers-like. With horses that always get quicker after a flying change, introduce the half circle for the change of rein in the middle of the long side and ride the flying change into the corner just before the end of the long side. The cor-ner should have a calming effect on the horse and help with the change.

the aids for the flying change, riding travers-like in the new direction, resulting hopefully in the flying change.

Serial changes on the circle

You can work on serial changes well by using shoulder-in and counter shoulder-in. Serial changes on the circle are most certainly the hardest type to ride, since they have to be ridden very straight on the line of the circle. For the horse this exercise is pleasant, since it is on a regular shape without corners, and can always keep the same rhythm when changing.

In order to ask the horse to change, you need to move from shoulder-in to counter canter and from counter shoulder-in to inside lead. Each change is caused by building up the shoulder-in or counter shoulder-in. Later, this change in flexion is ridden flatter and flatter so that you only need to change the bend slightly in order to get the flying change. At the same time, this method has the advantage of allowing you to ride flying changes through corners without stress or interruption.

Problem solving

Changing late behind

Changing late behind, meaning the inside hindleg is late to change, is often caused by the rider sitting incorrectly inside and back in the saddle. But also if the horse is ridden either too quickly, or with too little collection, then the hindleg can be too slow and come through too late.

Often the only correction needed is for the rider to work on the quality of the canter, asking for a greater degree of difference between collected and extended canter. By doing this the horse will gain in rhythm and the ability to collect. Then collect the canter as much as possible and ride the change more forwards without allowing the horse to run off. Before the next change, slow down the tempo again, increase the collection and again ride forwards into the next flying change.

If the problem persists, then you will need to make the hindquarters faster, in the true sense of the word. To do this, ride travers on the circle from A or C in canter. Just before reaching X, move the quarters across to the outside and change the circle, resulting in renvers – which will cause the horse to change behind first. Then the rider should open the new inside rein, giving a half-halt on the new outside rein to complete the change. This method can also be used to prepare more nervy horses for flying changes. The lateral movement makes it virtually impossible for the horse to take off.

Later you can try riding straight across the diagonal and move the quarters to the outside, which changes the horse's bend and causes the horse to change behind first. This exercise is also very well suited to correct a horse that tends to change late when doing successive changes.

Changing late in front

This mistake will usually only occur if the rider is holding the reins too tightly and restricting the horse's shoulders. In rare cases the rider may be gripping so hard with his knees that the shoulder is so restricted in its movement it actually prevents the horse's forehand from changing through correctly.

When the quality of the canter is good and the horse has developed sufficient strength, then the problem of changing late behind usually solves itself.

Using the **pirouette** for bend

This chapter deals particularly with the canter pirouette, which is a movement that relies on balance and the ability to collect in canter. To make matters more complicated, the horse must also be bent through the ribs. As with so many facets of riding, for this movement there is more than one way of getting there. You just have to look at where your own horse's weaknesses are and start from there.

Bending through the ribs is rarely the only problem when difficulties are encountered with the pirouette. By quietly working in travers on a circle and with a little patience, the difficulties can be quickly overcome.

Nothing will happen without bend through the ribs

Most horses have weaknesses caused by the carrying power of the hindquarters. Other problems might also occur but these are symptoms of the main problem. A horse may, for example get stiffer through its ribs during the pirouette, so our first thought is to work working on the bend through the ribs. If, however, you are interested in biomechanics, then you will know that a horse that isn't ridden through from behind and isn't using its hindquarters properly, he cannot bend properly through his ribs.

In no other movement is the bend through the ribs as important as in the pirouette – though unfortunately, bend through the ribs is often confused with neck flexion. Alternatively, people think that a neck that is bent sharply has a positive effect on the ribs. It's quite the opposite though – the horse is more likely to be straight through his ribs, because due to the bend in the neck the outside shoulder is opened and the energy coming from the quarters is lost through the open shoulder.

These observations confirm what I have always said: that in most cases the ribs remain straight because the inside hindleg doesn't push through. You can see this in the half-pass: if at the end of a half-pass both flexion and bend are lost and the rider courageously continues to drive with the inside leg, the impulsion is re-activated and with it also the bend.

> The saddle too can be the cause of problems with the bend. When the horse is asked for extreme degrees of bend, the panels of the saddle can slip so much that they might press quite painfully into the vertebrae of the spine and the horse may then refuse to work. (See page 30)

Riding triangles and squares

To improve the ability of the horse to step under itself and as further preparation for the pirouette, riding on a square is an ideal exercise. You need to ride on a square that is set about 2 metres in from the track. Position a cone in each corner for guidance. Walk on a straight line that goes to the outside of the cone, riding until the horse's quarters are on a line with the cone. Then flex the horse with the inside rein and contain the outside shoulder with the outside rein so that the forehand moves around the hindquarters in a quarter pirouette. Later you can ask the horse to work around a cone in a demi pirouette.

At every turn the horse needs to bring his weight back on to his hindquarters, and can then relax on the straight line that follows. Before every turn the rider has the opportunity to actively push the horse through up under his centre of gravity. If the horse manages the exercise in walk then I would begin the same exercise in trot. It is important to remember that the rider needs to sit balanced, and only lead the horse around the corners using half-halts on the outside rein. All attempts to use force to pull the horse around the corner will only cause the horse to lose his balance and fall back into walk. A rider that has never felt what it is like to have a horse that dances under the saddle will discover the key in this exercise.

The cones help the rider to ride triangles and squares more accurately.

The path towards unseen aids ...

...is the dream of every dedicated rider. And it is actually a contradiction, as often it is not that the observer can't see the aids, but rather a case of the rider simply not giving any aids. If you were now to accuse me of launching into romantic rhetoric then you are wrong: the prerequisite for achieving these so-called invisible aids is a relaxed horse that is alert, motivated and supple. Again and again the horse's own

emotional state is forgotten about: a horse that is capable of dance-like movement doesn't achieve it out of a sense of fear. A certain degree of excitement is necessary and even helpful, but the horse shouldn't begin to run away. Especially with the lateral movements, providing the preparation is done correctly, this goal can be reached.

In practice, work leading up to this could look like this: by touching the hindleg gently with the whip repeatedly whilst

The turns cause the horse to transfer more weight back and to sit more on his hindquarters.

playing lightly with the reins the walk can be influenced so that the horse begins to take shortened steps but with plenty of swing. Repeat this with more intensity, but stop when the horse starts to almost break into trot, so as not to cause stress. The walk and trot that this type of work can develop are much brighter and very balanced, but the horse is much more sensitive to the aids. If the lateral movements are well established in walk, then it should suffice just to think of the aids, or at least sit in the correct position, and take up the appropriate rein and the horse should begin to move laterally in the correct direction.

Perfecting collection
using piaffe and passage

Piaffe and passage can be wonderful tools for improving a horse's paces and expression. Some experts argue about when piaffe should be taught. In my opinion, the right time has come when the piaffe can help a horse the most, and when it is far enough advanced in both its training and the development of its personality. Even a four-year-old horse can benefit from being worked towards piaffe, and as a result will find collected movements easier, out of which can be developed a way of going that leads to a successful competition career. This applies not just to dressage horses, but also to western horses that can gain in lightness and balance in the western disciplines.

This piaffe is pace-like, since the rider is gripping with his legs. For the initial steps of piaffe the rider is just the passenger!

The path to piaffe

I prefer two ways of working towards piaffe. Either I walk alongside the rider while they work working in shoulder-in in walk or trot, with a whip, or I work the horse in-hand using long-reins or double lunge lines.

If the piaffe is established, the rider should have patience and use it first, before trying to develop the passage too early. Otherwise there is the danger that the horse goes into passage

without using his back properly, resulting in him not being able to go back into piaffe because he hasn't developed either enough strength or the correct technique.

In my opinion, it is better to start the piaffe work early, but to work on it for at least six months-using transitions between half-step piaffe and piaffe on the spot. It is precisely these transitions that can improve a horse's paces and help it to

Offering the support of someone on the ground, using a whip alongside the rider's aids, is one way of working towards piaffe. By using shoulder-in, less energy is trapped between the hands and seat and the horse stays more relaxed for the first steps of piaffe.

improve its balance, so that in the harder movements it gains in expression and the movements are more secure.

Even between the basic paces, correct transitions are one of the most important goals of training. In the chapter on the rein-back, the aid to ask the horse to 'sit' back on its haunches is described a using the leg that is brought back. If you tend to ride sensitive horses using frequent transitions between walk and trot, as well as working trot to collected trot using the same drawn back leg, then the horse will get more and more dance-like in its movement until half-steps result. Over time this can be developed into the piaffe, where the horse really sits on its quarters. In order to get the horse to sit back on his quarters in piaffe, you will need to go back to riding halt and rein-back using your legs drawn back.

A perfect transition to passage: the rider is sitting up, without pushing.

Working towards passage

For me, the passage is always a product of the piaffe – meaning the passage results from riding forwards, virtually an extension from the piaffe.

I am usually called upon to assist in the training of piaffe amongst sports horses that have been trained to passage first of all, which will often have been developed out of the extended trot. This often results in the rider having to strug-

gle with hindquarters that aren't working correctly. The beginnings of piaffe are then difficult because the horse tends to take steps that are tense between the moments of suspension, but does not sit back on his quarters properly and is not working through his back. The same applies to horses that perform in shows and are often asked to passage out of Spanish walk. The result is that the

If the passage is developed correctly then the hindleg stays active.

horse concentrates too much on the forehand and forgets about the hindquarters.

The passage is correctly developed from piaffe by building the piaffe up on the spot and then using this stored energy by asking the horse to go forwards for as long as the hindquarters keep the rhythm. The passage is therefore developed forwards out of piaffe. It is best to ask a helper to walk alongside you with a stick. But be careful – the helper should only help and not put the horse under stress by using the whip too much, otherwise the horse may react by kicking out.

A few final words

Every horse and every person is different. It isn't possible to write a book in which every problem that arises between horse and rider is explained. Nor can the correct order of exercises be set in stone, since this too depends upon the individual's own strengths and weaknesses. A rider's most important tools are feeling and consistency in the way they act, and that means sometimes being tough when necessary, but always being fair and predictable. Predictability and consistency are the basis of a healthy life in a herd, and also to achieve for the true 'coming together as one' of horse and rider in movement.

Riding means being creative every day, and again and again interpreting what you are learning from riding correctly. A rider should never put his feelings behind the sometimes doubtful dogma that comes from so much of the riding world. A movement that feels or looks hard or unpleasant will never result in harmony and refinement, but will always lead to stress and irritation.

You should never forget that a rider without a horse is just a person – but a horse without a rider is still a horse!

Thanks

I would like to give a big thank you to all my pupils who have allowed themselves to be photographed for this book:

- Ernst Ulmerich with his Friesian stallion Jelde
- Andrea Mönninghoff, Equestrian centre Diekhof with her Friesian stallion Jabe
- Family Hellmayr from the Horse Training Center Hellmayr with her Friesian
- Franz Tiefenthaler with his warmblood mare Germania
- Elisabeth Walentin with her warmblood mare Lady Lu
- Kerstin Gellner with her warmblood mare Francine
- Irmgard Oberlaber with her Andalusian gelding Inquisitor.

In addition, my deepest thanks go to the photographer Christiane Slawik, who carried out her work with so much attention to detail and creativity.

References

Neindorff, Egon von:
The Art of Classical Horsemanship
Cadmos Books, 2009

Podhajski, Alois:
Horsemanship: A Comprehensive Book on Training the Horse and Its Rider
J.A. Allen, 2003

Steinbrecht, Gustav:
The Gymnasium of the Horse
Xenophon Press, 1995

Ziegner, Kurt Albrecht von:
Elements of Dressage
Cadmos Books, 2002

CADMOS
HORSE GUIDES

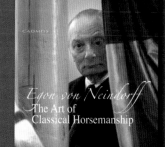

Egon von Neindorff
THE ART OF CLASSICAL HORSEMANSHIP

Egon von Neindorff dedicated his life to the kn
and promotion of the classical art of riding. He
understood the philosophy of classical riding a
therefore able to teach his students to develop
own style. The essence of classical dressage
a deep affection for the horse, understanding,
tivity, humility and devotion. In this book, von N
illustrates in more than thirty chapters his prof
understanding of the natural training of horses
encompasses a body of knowledge, which wa
viously only taught at his riding establishment
Karlsruhe.

272 pages
Hardcover, full colour
ISBN 978-3-86127-919-8

Thies Böttcher
GENTLE HORSE TRAINING

'The rider is the horse's trainer.'
Adopting this underlying principle to his training, Thies Böttcher shows how to develop
your horse's abilities and advance his training,
using simple but effective methods. The foundation for this work is to understand how a
horse learns, and to apply this knowledge
throughout the training process. Divided into
four modules, this training approach can be
worked through over four months, and can be
easily integrated into your training programme,
whatever your style of riding.

144 pages
Softcover, full colour
ISBN 978-3-86127-977-8

Kurd Albrecht von Ziegner
ELEMENTS
OF DRESSAGE

This book was developed to help riders,
trainers and judges understand what it
takes to classically train a horse so it
can succeed in any discipline. The au-
thor presents the 'Training Tree', a con-
cept that is compelling, and easy to
understand. It outlines the ten essential
elements of classical basic training and
shows how the elements are related and
in what order they should be achieved.

128 pages
Softcover, full colour
ISBN 978-3-86127-902-0

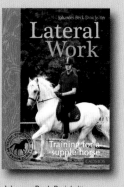

Johannes Beck-Broichsitter
LATERAL WORK

Lateral work is an essential part of any
training programme leading to a supple
horse. This book offers a step-by-step
guide through all of the lateral movements, introducing exercises to prepare
horse and rider for the first lateral movements, through to training exercises, as
well as stretching and loosening exercises.

128 pages
Softcover, full colour
ISBN 978-3-86127-973-0

Jean-Claude Racinet
FALLING FOR FALLACIES

The world of modern dressage includes an ent
canon of doctrines, which are never questione
either individually or in form of the system, whi
they present in their entirety. However, what d
really mean to drive the horse 'onto the bit'? D
stronger application of the rider's aids really en
age the horse to place its hind legs further und
body? Jean-Claude Racinet subjects these and
other questions to a critical analysis and unco
many contradictions. This book, a summary of
des of extensive experiences as a rider, offers
long-overdue contribution towards the discuss
of the sense and nonsense of the training doct
It deals effectively with prejudices and is aime
supporting the art of horse-orientated equitatio

160 pages
Hardcover, full colour
ISBN 978-3-86127-969-3

For more information, please visit: **www.cadmos.co.uk**